WOMEN
IN THE
RESISTANCE

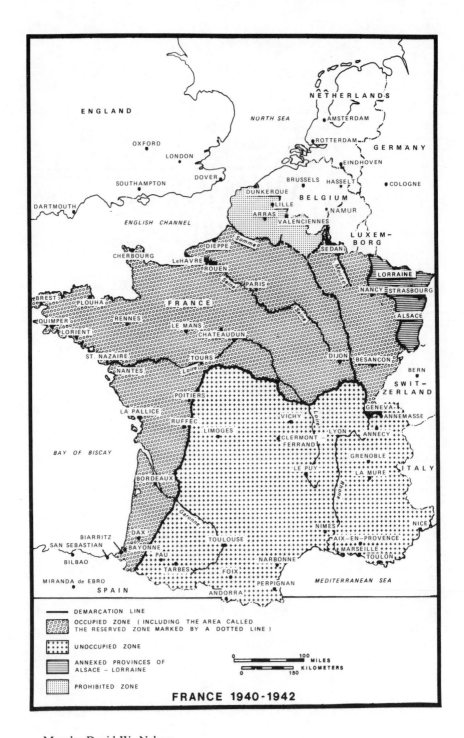

FRANCE 1940-1942

DEMARCATION LINE

OCCUPIED ZONE (INCLUDING THE AREA CALLED
THE RESERVED ZONE MARKED BY A DOTTED LINE)

UNOCCUPIED ZONE

ANNEXED PROVINCES OF
ALSACE - LORRAINE

PROHIBITED ZONE

100 MILES
150 KILOMETERS

Map by David W. Nelson

WOMEN
IN THE
RESISTANCE

Margaret L. Rossiter

PRAEGER SPECIAL STUDIES • PRAEGER SCIENTIFIC

New York • Philadelphia • Eastbourne, UK
Toronto • Hong Kong • Tokyo • Sydney

12311880
DLC

12-1-97

Library of Congress Cataloging-in-Publication Data

Rossiter, Margaret L.
  Women in the resistance.

  Bibliography: p.
  Includes index.
  1. World War, 1939–1945 – Underground movements –
France. 2. World War, 1939–1945 – Women – France.
3. France – History – German occupation, 1940–1945.
I. Title.
D802. F8R595   1985   940.53′44   85-16746
ISBN   0-03-005338-2   (alk. paper)
ISBN   0-03-005339-0   (pbk. : alk paper)

Published in 1986 by Praeger Publishers
CBS Educational and Professional Publishing, a Division of CBS Inc.
521 Fifth Avenue, New York, NY 10175 USA

© 1986 by Praeger Publishers

6789   052   987654321

Printed in the United States of America on acid-free paper

INTERNATIONAL OFFICES

Orders from outside the United States should be sent to the appropriate address listed below. Orders from areas not
listed below should be placed through CBS International Publishing. 383 Madison Ave., New York, NY 10175 USA

Australia, New Zealand
Holt Saunders. Pty. Ltd.. 9 Waltham St.. Artarmon. N.S.W. 2064. Sydney, Australia

Canada
Holt. Rinehart & Winston of Canada, 55 Horner Ave.. Toronto, Ontario, Canada M8Z 4X6

Europe, the Middle East, & Africa
Holt Saunders. Ltd.. 1 St. Anne's Road. Eastbourne. East Sussex, England BN21 3UN

Japan
Holt Saunders. Ltd.. Ichibancho Central Building. 22-1 Ichibancho. 3rd Floor, Chiyodaku, Tokyo, Japan

Hong Kong, Southeast Asia
Holt Saunders Asia. Ltd.. 10 Fl. Intercontinental Plaza, 94 Granville Road, Tsim Sha Tsui East, Kowloon,
Hong Kong

**Manuscript submissions should be sent to the Editorial Director, Praeger Publishers, 521 Fifth Avenue,
New York, NY 10175 USA**

TO MY HUSBAND, TED

CONTENTS

PREFACE

Although many women were engaged in the underground struggle to liberate France from the German occupation, the names of relatively few have figured in accounts of the French resistance. My purpose in writing this book has been to find out more about the part women played in the various resistance groups and to evaluate not only their contribution to the Nazi defeat but also its possible effect on the political status of French women. Did it, for example, have any bearing on their being enfranchised in 1944?

Information about women participants in the clandestine operations described here was difficult to obtain, and bits and pieces of their stories had to be gleaned from many sources. Books and articles by or about some individual heroines in the resistance have appeared, and I have drawn on those published sources to some extent. But a great deal of the material here comes directly from my interviews and correspondence with individuals who took part in the resistance or can speak authoritatively about it. I also include hitherto unpublished information uncovered in my searches through military and other government records, and the reports of private organizations in the United States and abroad.

Beginning in 1974, I interviewed 64 women and 36 men in France, England, Belgium, and the United States, almost all of whom permitted me to tape-record their recollections of events.[1] Some of those interviewed volunteered to lend me unpublished memoirs and other documents from their personal archives. In the course of this study I also corresponded with more than 100 former members of resistance groups and with other well-informed people. They answered countless questions, and 23 sent me extensive information.[2]

In addition, I read the *témoignages* (statements) that many resisters made in interviews conducted soon after the war under the auspices of the Comité d'Histoire de la Deuxième Guerre Mondiale in Paris.[3]

Information also turned up in the collection of clandestine newspapers at the Bibliothèque Nationale, and in a few documents at the Bibliothèque Marguerite Durand in Paris and at the Bibliothèque de la Documentation Internationale Contemporaine at Nanterre. Documents about some OSS women, missions, and intelligence chains in France were acquired from the Central

Intelligence Agency under the Freedom of Information Act, but only after a delay of four years.

As my research advanced, I discovered that the best available documents about women in the resistance were those describing their work in escape lines. Reports from U.S. servicemen who received help from escape lines are in the National Archives, Washington National Records Center, in Suitland, Maryland.[4] Chapters 2, 3, and 4 of this book contain much detail drawn from the 3,000 firsthand accounts of downed American airmen who evaded capture or escaped from German hands and managed to return to England thanks to the help of resistance networks. The stories the soldiers told in their interrogations by army intelligence officers contain a wealth of information about women who fed and sheltered them, and often guided them on their way to the next safehouse.

For security reasons, evaders usually knew their benefactors only by their pseudonyms or first names, but I was able to trace many individuals through materials compiled by the tripartite Awards Bureau, set up in Paris while the war was still in progress in an effort to identify the civilian patriots who had risked their lives to help Allied aviators.[5] The American section began functioning in October 1944 with a card file of about 3,000 names picked up from the escape and evasion reports.

Identifying the people who dared not give their real names to the men they were helping was a major problem for the Awards Bureau, but when one person was traced, the trail might lead to three or four others. The French press cooperated by urging anyone with information about escape lines to report the facts to the Awards Bureau. Once helpers were located, they were asked to fill out questionnaires describing their work, identifying the airmen they helped, and naming others in the group. Official recognition of resisters had to begin at the local level, with a declaration by the individual, which was then sent to the organization's headquarters.[6] American awards in the form of the newly established Medal of Freedom, letters of appreciation, or financial reimbursement were based on some 5,000 dossiers, many of which are now in the Washington National Records Center, along with detailed histories by American intelligence officers about some of the largest escape lines.

The intelligence records in the Washington National Records Center were made available to me under Executive Order 11652 of 1972, which provided that security classified information would be declassified after 30 years under certain conditions. The documents were subject to review for security and for information that might constitute an invasion of privacy; they were declassified as I requested them.

Information about women engaged in other kinds of work for the resistance is harder to find, and the same difficulties arise concerning their identity. During the many months spent sifting through records, I was constantly aware that all the networks included valiant women who received no official recognition, particularly those in the lower echelons who could devote only part of their time to the cause.

More people and organizations have helped with this book than I can acknowledge here. My greatest thanks go to the diminishing band of men and women who served the resistance and generously gave me information that I could get nowhere else. Many received me in their homes. Others wrote and talked to me by telephone. In particular instances their information helped me to clear up misconceptions created in earlier accounts.

Research in France and the United States was made possible in part by grants from the American Philosophical Society and the Josephine Keal Fund. The staffs of several institutions greatly aided my research. At the Comité d'Histoire de la Deuxième Guerre Mondiale, Henri Michel, the secretary-general, made suggestions about sources and gave me access to the archives; Françoise Mercier, archivist, and Michel Rauzier, librarian, provided me with documents and books. In the United States at the National Archives, John Taylor of the Modern Military Branch not only provided me with many military and OSS documents, but also put me in touch with people associated with the OSS. At the Washington National Records Center, archivists George Chalou and Frederick Pernell were most cooperative in providing me with essential documents. My cousin Virginia Giltner performed valuable services by searching through countless boxes of evasion records at the WNRC.

At Eastern Michigan University the library staff obtained many books through interlibrary loan. My colleague Prof. Daryl Hafter made helpful suggestions about the organization and content of the book, and Prof. Brigitte Robert Muller assisted me with the translation of some French paragraphs into English; unattributed translations are my own. One of my former students, Carole Edgerton, translated many letters into French and typed them as well. Constance Greenbaum, who is now working on a thesis at the University of Paris, served as my research assistant. In addition to checking documents, she helped to locate resisters for whom I was searching and interviewed five people in my stead.

Ralph Patton, president of the Air Forces Escape and Evasion Society, provided me with a great deal of material. In addition, 132 members of the society (60 percent) responded to my questionnaire asking for details about important assistance given to them by women. Pierre Bauset, president of the Royal Air Forces Escaping Society, Canadian Branch, also contributed information.

Special thanks are due Rosannah Steinhoff of Ann Arbor, who read the entire manuscript and made valuable suggestions about its organization and style. Arlene Phillips of Eastern Michigan University was most cooperative in typing the manuscript. Finally, I want to thank my editors at Praeger, Dotty Breitbart and Susan Alkana, who shepherded my manuscript through the various stages with enthusiasm and skill.

Notes

1. Their names are listed in the bibliography.

2. Their names are listed in the bibliography.

3. After the Comité went out of existence at the end of 1980, the *témoignages* and other documents, such as agents' reports, letters, and personal records, were transferred to the Archives Nationales. Staff members were transferred to the Institut d'Histoire du Temps Présent.

4. See Guide to Frequently Cited Sources.

5. The Awards Bureau represented the joint efforts of the U.S. Awards Section, P/W and X Detachment, G-2; the British MI 9; and the French Direction Générale d'Etudes et Recherches (DGER). In September 1944 the 6801 MIS-X Detachment was organized (but not activated until May 1945) to carry on the work of the U.S. Awards Section.

6. The DGER was interested in all types of resistance; the British and the Americans, only in escapes and evasions.

1 PRELUDE TO ACTION

1 FRANCE ON BERLIN TIME

Much is known about the resistance to the Nazi conqueror that developed throughout the country after France's defeat by Germany in 1940, but the part played by women has not been adequately recorded. This book will tell the story of what women did in the resistance: how they rescued Allied airmen shot down by the Germans by serving as leaders, hostesses, and guides of escape lines, thus making it possible for airmen to return to their bases in England, and how they gathered military intelligence, managed clandestine newspapers, and carried out sabotage and guerrilla operations. Women served in all capacities from typists to organizers and chiefs of resistance networks. As "combattantes sans uniforme" they helped immeasurably to undermine the foundations of the German occupation and hasten the defeat of the enemy.

The part women played in the resistance will be best understood against the background of events that began with the German invasion of the Netherlands and Belgium on May 10, 1940. The blitzkrieg of the German Panzer divisions abruptly ended the "phony war" that had existed on the Western Front since the Nazi conquest of Poland in September 1939. French armies and the British Expeditionary Force (BEF) rushed to support the Belgians in accordance with the French War Plan and in response to a last-minute appeal from King Leopold, whose country had put its faith in neutrality.

The Allied defense plan was derailed when General von Kleist's Panzer group smashed through the supposedly impassable Belgian Ardennes and hurled two armored corps across the Meuse River in eastern France. General Guderian then raced with his armored divisions to the Channel coast. By this daring maneuver the Germans cut the Allied forces in two. The Belgian army and the supporting British and French troops were caught in a net. Efforts to break out failed, and the weary Belgians surrendered on May 27,

1940.[1] The BEF and remnants of three French armies were forced back to Dunkerque.

During 9 frantic days, from May 26 to June 4, rescuers plucked 338,226 soldiers from the beaches in what was called the "miracle of Dunkerque." Almost 200,000 of these were British; the rest, French and Belgian. This gallant action had its repercussions, however. Although 130,000 trapped French soldiers had been saved at Dunkerque by an impromptu fleet of British and French ships, the French were bitterly aware that 40,000 others were left to be taken prisoner by the Germans. They firmly believed that the British had withdrawn prematurely from the Continent, leaving them to face the enemy alone.[2]

There was no respite after Dunkerque. On June 5 Hitler opened the Battle of France by unleashing 100 divisions in a mighty 4-pronged attack. The Germans advanced so rapidly, supported by the Luftwaffe, that the French had little time for effective counterattack. On June 10, sensing that France was about to fall and hoping to gain credit with his Axis partner, the fascist dictator Mussolini declared war on France.

Shaken by these events, the French cabinet, led by Premier Paul Reynaud, abruptly left Paris and moved to Tours. On June 14 the Germans triumphantly entered an almost deserted capital, which had been declared an open city, and raced toward the Loire River. The French government withdrew to Bordeaux in southwestern France.

Meanwhile, Premier Reynaud and British Prime Minister Winston Churchill made desperate efforts to keep France in the war. Churchill supported the usually energetic French premier. Reynaud, at first backed by a majority of his cabinet, believed that if the German offensive could not be halted, the French government should go to North Africa to continue the war. He was opposed by his new supreme commander, Gen. Maxime Weygand, and by his vice-premier, the 84-year-old Marshal Henri Philippe Pétain, the World War I hero of Verdun. They insisted that the government remain in France and seek an armistice.[3]

By June 16 the French armies were collapsing. On the same day Churchill, in a last-ditch effort to head off a capitulation by the French, supported a dramatic plan of Franco-British union. The terms of the plan were telephoned to Reynaud by Brig. Gen. Charles de Gaulle, his undersecretary for national defense, who was in London conferring with Churchill. Reynaud immediately took the proposal to his cabinet, but without success. His colleagues were suspicious of the British motives; and in any case they believed the situation was hopeless. Reynaud resigned in despair.[4]

He was promptly replaced by Marshal Pétain, who was appointed premier by Albert Lebrun, president of the Third Republic. In his radio address to the people, Pétain praised the army for fighting with a heroism worthy of its traditions against an enemy superior in number and arms. Then he said:

"I give to France the gift of my person to attenuate her misfortune. . . . It is with a heavy heart that I say to you today that the fighting must cease." He then added that he had asked the Germans for an armistice.[5]

Many French troops, hearing reports about the marshal's speech, believed that the war was over. They threw down their weapons and joined the exodus of several million people choking the roads as they fled before the Germans. Most French civilians were relieved that the fighting was over. Marie Madeleine Fourcade, who became a prominent resistance leader, reported: "Women smiled, people kissed one another. In the cafes the crowds drank to the health of the old marshal."[6] Young Brigitte Robert, a secretary in the Commerce Department in Paris, who moved with the government to Vichy, remarked that "our army had been defeated and the fighting had to stop. There was an instinctive feeling of relief."[7]

At the same time the French were stunned by the humiliating debacle after only six weeks of fighting. They had believed in their army, supposedly the best in Europe, and the security of the Maginot Line. Military collapse was a new and traumatic experience. Like many others, Marie Madeleine Fourcade felt an immense wave of anguish engulf her.

The armistice terms imposed by a jubilant Hitler on June 22 were severe. France would be divided into occupied and unoccupied zones, with a rigid demarcation line between the two. The Germans would directly control three-fifths of the country, an area that included northern and western France and the entire Atlantic coast. The remaining section of the country would be administered by the French government under Marshal Pétain.[8]

According to other provisions of the armistice, the French army would be disbanded except for a force of 100,000 men to maintain domestic order; France would pay the occupation costs of German troops;[9] the French government would prevent members of its armed forces from leaving the country and forbid its citizens to fight against the Germans. The government was also required to surrender upon demand any Germans living in France, most of whom were Jews. Pending the conclusion of a peace treaty, French prisoners of war, numbering approximately 1.5 million, would remain in captivity. By this decree thousands of women were left without husbands, brothers, or sons and had strong reason to join the later resistance.

One of the armistice terms posed a special threat to Great Britain. The Germans demanded that the French navy, the second most powerful in Europe, be interned in ports under Axis control. Although Hitler pledged not to use the fleet, the British questioned the value of such an assurance. If the Germans seized the French navy, it could mean the defeat of the English in the approaching Battle of Britain. Churchill, deciding that the risk was too great, ordered a naval force to Mers-el-Kebir, Algeria, where the French Atlantic squadron was berthed. The British sealed off the harbor with mines and then delivered an ultimatum giving the French commander three choices:

to fight with the British, to sail to British ports to be interned, or to sail to French Caribbean bases. When the ultimatum was rejected on July 3, the British opened fire on the French squadron, killing 1,267 sailors and sinking all but one cruiser and three destroyers. A wave of anti-British indignation swept across France, and the Pétain government broke diplomatic relations with its recent ally.[10]

By this time the French government had transferred to Vichy, a small resort city in unoccupied France noted for its mineral springs. There the Chamber of Deputies and the Senate of the Third Republic, in joint session as the National Assembly, gave Pétain full powers to draft a new constitution. The vote, a lopsided 569 to 80, indicated the revulsion that the members of Parliament, numbed with shock, felt against the republic that had brought them to defeat. Conversely, it showed their hope for strong leadership from Pétain, who became head of the French state.[11]

The old marshal was a father figure. He reminded the people that he had been with them in the glorious days of the past and that he would remain with them in the somber days of the present. He urged them to stay at his side and he would atone for the country's misfortune.[12] Like many other conservatives, Pétain believed that France had been defeated because of its lack of discipline and zeal. France was guilty of laxness, and the defeat was therefore merited. Suzanne Borel, who was attached to the Office of Information in Vichy, ironically summed up the government's attitude: "We were defeated, but with honor. It wasn't our fault; it was the fault of the English, the Jews, the unpatriotic schoolteachers. Of course it was not the fault of the generals. It was a kind of morphine."[13]

For two years the Vichy regime acted as a partial screen between the French in the unoccupied zone and the Germans. Here the conqueror was not visible, as he was in the north and west, and many believed that Pétain would save France from the terrible fate of Poland. Others were convinced that the marshal was playing a double game by only pretending to collaborate with the Germans. Was it not realistic to adopt a policy of *attentisme* — to wait and see what developed?

Meanwhile, however, another army officer, Charles de Gaulle, was following a dramatically different path. An exponent of mechanized warfare, he had been promoted to brigadier general in May 1940 because of his aggressive use of tanks against the Germans. At age 49 he was the youngest general in the French army when his old friend Premier Reynaud appointed him undersecretary for national defense. De Gaulle feared that it might be too late to win the Battle of France, but he forcefully advocated a fighting retreat to Brittany and the later transfer of the government and armed forces to French North Africa.[14]

Because of de Gaulle's determination to continue the fight, Reynaud sent him to London on June 16 to ask Churchill for help in transporting

French troops to North Africa. He was also to urge Churchill to support the Anglo-French plan of union, and thus strengthen Reynaud's hand in dealing with the growing number of advisers who insisted on an armistice.[15]

Having completed this mission, de Gaulle flew to Bordeaux in a plane provided by Churchill. There he learned from his aides that Reynaud had resigned and that President Lebrun had asked Pétain to form a new government. Knowing that this meant "certain capitulation," de Gaulle decided to leave France the next morning. Because his wife and children would be endangered when he left the country, he arranged for them to join him in England. On June 17 he arrived in London on the plane lent to him by Churchill, feeling, he said, "like a man on the shore of an ocean proposing to swim across."[16]

The view from England was grim. German armies had conquered Poland in 26 days, Norway in 28 days, Denmark in 24 hours, the Netherlands in 5 days, Belgium in 18 days, and now France in an unbelievable 42 days. Britain was expected to be the next victim, and hardly anyone believed that the British could stop the Nazi tide.

Despite these successes of the German juggernaut, de Gaulle was determined to muster what forces he could against the invaders. He conferred with Churchill, who agreed to put the BBC at his disposal. On June 18 the young general delivered his famous appeal to the French:

> Speaking in full knowledge of the facts, I ask you to believe me when I say that the cause of France is not lost. . . . This war is not limited to one unfortunate country. The outcome of the struggle has not been decided by the Battle of France. This is a world war. . . . Today we are crushed by the sheer weight of mechanized force hurled against us, but we can still look to a future in which even greater mechanized force will bring us to victory. The destiny of the world is at stake.
>
> I, General de Gaulle, now in London, call on all French officers and men who are at present on British soil, or may be in the future, with or without their arms; I call on all engineers and skilled workmen from the armament factories who are at present on British soil, or may be in the future, to get in touch with me.
>
> Whatever happens, the flame of French resistance must not and shall not die.[17]

De Gaulle wanted to set up a military force of French soldiers and sailors to continue the fight against the Germans. He wanted his compatriots to understand that even though Pétain had capitulated, the war would go on and eventually they would be victorious. Since he was the first to use the word "resistance," his speech marked the birth of the resistance outside of France and inspired many patriots within the country.

As it turned out, the French resistance was not limited to military action.

It would include all activities that violated the German and Italian armistice agreements.[18] It would also include underground action taken in defiance of enemy and Vichy decrees in France. Resistance therefore ranged from chalking "V for Victory" signs on sidewalks to fighting guerrilla actions against the Germans.

At first only a few volunteers joined de Gaulle in London, partly because he was not well known. Fully aware of this handicap, de Gaulle offered to serve under higher-ranking French army officers if they would reject the armistice and come to London. When no one accepted his offer, de Gaulle picked up the mantle and was recognized by the British government on June 28 as "leader of the Free French." This action infuriated the Vichy regime, which ordered de Gaulle to return to France to be tried for desertion. A month later a court martial condemned him to death in absentia.[19]

Few people in France heard de Gaulle's "Appeal of June 18," but many nevertheless made the perilous decision not to accept defeat. They were offended by the craven surrender and the presence of German troops in their country. They were indignant that huge swastika flags flew from the public buildings and monuments of Paris, including the Arc de Triomphe, which had been commissioned by Napoleon. They were annoyed that the clocks in occupied France were advanced to German summer time.

Feeling both angry and frustrated, some patriots met with friends to discuss what to do. They spontaneously formed small groups that responded to immediate needs. In the occupied zone they helped French and British prisoners of war and Jews to escape across the demarcation line to the south of France, and they collected military intelligence about the German armed forces. In both zones such groups provided food and shelter for fugitives, made false identity cards, collected and hid weapons, and wrote and distributed underground leaflets and newspapers. Gradually, they established contact with others to become part of a resistance *réseau* (network). By 1943 a complex web of networks extended across France.

How resistance groups evolved into networks can be illustrated by the experience of Germaine Tillion, a 33-year-old French anthropologist, who helped to organize and federate early resistance groups in occupied France. Shortly before the French capitulation, Tillion had returned to Paris from a scientific study of the Berbers in Algeria. Deciding that they must do something about the German occupation, she and some of her friends met to plan their moves. They were all amateurs and had to invent the structure of the resistance, but they quickly became effective. In August 1940 Tillion organized evasion groups by obtaining the addresses of places where the demarcation line could be crossed without the special German pass required under the new regime. She also obtained names of people who would house and feed evaders or furnish them with false papers. The first to be aided by her were French prisoners of war in temporary detention camps in France and Jews trying to flee the country.[20]

During this early effort Tillion was approached by a 74-year-old retired army colonel, Paul Hauet. A graduate of the Ecole Polytechnique and a World War I veteran, Hauet was director of the Union National des Combattants Coloniaux, an organization officially involved in providing food for French African and Asian prisoners of war held in German camps in France. He permitted Tillion to use the offices of the Union for organizing a resistance group. She recruited teams of men and women who could tell the prisoners in their own language how they might escape.[21]

Tillion and Hauet were joined by Col. Duthiel de La Rochère, also a graduate of the Ecole Polytechnique and a veteran of World War I. The two retired officers had met by accident under curious circumstances. Soon after the occupation the Germans had used sledgehammers and dynamite to destroy a statue of Gen. Charles Mangin, a World War I hero, charging that the general had provided German prostitutes for African troops during the French occupation of the Rhineland following the French victory in 1918. Drawn to the scene of the wreckage, the two colonels had fallen into conversation, and together decided that they must take action against the enemy.[22]

Since La Rochère wanted to concentrate on military intelligence, he and Hauet set up separate intelligence sections to collect and send information to England about the German armed forces. Tillion gave the two officers any items of intelligence that came to her attention, and in turn they gave her information about escape lines. It was easier to collect intelligence, however, than to send it to England, and La Rochère's next task was to look for another group that had contact with the British.[23] Tillion also aided in this project.

She was by this time involved not only with her own resistance groups and the Hauet-La Rochère groups, but also with friends at the Musée de l'Homme. This museum still occupies one of the two curving pavilions of the Palais de Chaillot, and between them lies the vast esplanade where a triumphant Hitler was photographed with the Eiffel Tower as a backdrop.

The director of the museum, Paul Rivet, had returned from an assignment in Colombia; Germaine Tillion knew that he and his close associates were fervently anti-fascist, and that they especially condemned the racial theories of the Nazis. In fact, as she found out, members of the museum staff were already taking steps against the Germans. Yvonne Oddon, the head librarian, had sent books and clothes to French prisoners of war in camps near Paris. With a friend, Mme Lucie Boutillier du Rétail, she had also helped some prisoners to escape and provided shelter, food, and information about routes across the demarcation line.[24]

Other staff members joining in the resistance efforts included Boris Vildé, a linguist, and Anatole Lewitsky, an anthropologist. The two men were Russian-born, naturalized French citizens who had served in the French army. They helped prisoners of war and Jews to escape, but they also planned to write and circulate propaganda leaflets and a newspaper opposing all collaboration with the enemy; they also hoped to send military intelligence to London. Vildé made contact with a British intelligence agent, and by the end of August the resistance group in the Musée de l'Homme was in full swing.[25]

Meanwhile Colonel de La Rochère, who was still looking for a way to transmit his intelligence and that of Hauet to London, heard of Yvonne Oddon through someone in the American embassy. He offered to give her intelligence about the German armed forces if she could dispatch it to England. She checked with Vildé and Lewitsky, and they agreed to relay the information from the colonel. Since La Rochère had served in Africa, he was made a member of the Société des Africainistes, a good cover for his trips to the library of the museum.[26] Despite their precautions, however, members of the museum group were arrested between February and April 1941. After de La Rochère and Hauet were arrested, on July 3, 1941, Germaine Tillion received the military intelligence from their agents and arranged for its transmission to England, first by the British and then by the Free French intelligence services.[27]

She knew that risks had to be taken if the German grip on France was to be loosened, and she continued to help create and federate groups. In 1941, through her friend Jacques Lecompte-Boinet, she was in touch with a resistance group led by Elisabeth Dussauze; and when the leaders of that group were arrested in February 1942, she helped Lecompte-Boinet set up a new group, Manipule. She also met with another intelligence group, SMH Gloria. It was because of her connection with Gloria that she was betrayed to the police by a double agent and arrested on August 13, 1942. After being imprisoned in France, she was deported to Ravensbrück, the notorious concentration camp for women.[28]

Because of the need for security, early resistance groups did not have names. After the war Germaine Tillion gave the name Musée de l'Homme to the loosely structured early network. Her first group, she explains, was a "patchwork" that was allied with the "patchwork Hauet" and the "patchwork La Rochère." La Rochère's group was sewed to the "patchwork Vildé," and these four groups became the *réseau* Musée de l'Homme, one of the most important of the early resistance.[29]

The Germans were too experienced as conquerors to delay letting the French know who was in charge in the occupied zone. They issued a proclamation on June 20 that followed the principle of a little carrot and a big stick. The people were to put their trust in the German army, which would guarantee their personal security. Those inhabitants who behaved peacefully would have nothing to fear. The systems supplying gas, electricity, and water, along with the railroads and national art treasures, were put under the protection of the German army. Any acts of violence and sabotage, including damage to German posters, would be punished.

A list of particular violations that would bring the accused before a military tribunal was added to the proclamation:

1. Assistance to Allied soldiers in the occupied zone
2. Aid to civilians trying to flee to unoccupied France
3. All transmission of intelligence to persons outside of the occupied territory
4. All connections with prisoners
5. All offenses against the German army and its chiefs
6. All public assemblies, demonstrations, and distribution of leaflets without the approval of the German authority
7. All work stoppages, whether in public services, the police, schools, or business enterprises.[30]

The German proclamation made it clear to everyone who refused to bow to the conqueror that acts of resistance would be dangerous. French citizens would be punished for such simple infractions as defacing German posters. But many were not cowed by Nazi threats. They believed that outwitting the police was a challenge and sometimes a game, even when the German decrees multiplied and the penalty became death or deportation.

In the occupied zone several police agencies confronted those who resisted. First there were the traditional French police, who were sometimes cooperative and sympathetic to the resistance. More dangerous were the German security agencies, such as the Abwehr of the German armed forces and the Sicherheitsdienst (SD) of the Schutzstaffel (SS). The Abwehr, under Adm. Wilhelm Canaris, had its Paris headquarters in the Hotel Lutétia on the boulevard Raspail. Its main branches were the Geheime Feldpolizei (GFP), the secret field police, whose chief function was to arrest suspects, and branch III, which was responsible for security, counterintelligence, and the liquidation of Allied agents. It had sections in the army, air force, and navy. It also placed agents in arms factories, railroad organizations, and the postal service, and it censored all domestic and foreign mail. This organization posed a special threat to resisters because it infiltrated double agents into their groups.[31]

The SD, under the notorious Heinrich Himmler, the head of the SS, had its Paris headquarters at 82-86 avenue Foch, within sight of the Arc de Triomphe. As Hitler's minister of the interior, Himmler also controlled the Geheime Staatspolizei (Gestapo), the secret state police. Its bleak headquarters were on the rue des Saussaies, in the gray building formerly occupied by the French Ministry of the Interior. The Gestapo and the SD had conflicting jurisdictions, and the responsibilities of both overlapped to some extent those of the Abwehr.[32]

As far as the French were concerned, the Abwehr, SD, and Gestapo were all lumped together and referred to with dread as the Gestapo. The men of the Gestapo were the ones who wore trench coats and drove around in black cars, and who knocked on doors at 4 A.M. to take resisters to the rue des Saussaies for harsh interrogation and imprisonment.

As long as only part of France was technically under occupation, the

German security services were not visible in the Vichy zone. They kept in the background, checking up on French gendarmes, many of whom were anti-German, and arranging the arrest of Allied agents. After the American and British landings in French North Africa in November 1942, Hitler's Axis partner, Mussolini, was permitted to occupy eight French administrative departments east of the Rhone River. Because the Italian secret police, the Organizzazione di Vigilanza e Repressione dell'Antifascismo (OVRA), did not share Hitler's enthusiasm for anti-Semitic decrees, Jews fared better in Italian-occupied France than elsewhere under the occupation, although the OVRA could also be brutal. When Mussolini fell from power in the summer of 1943, the Germans administered all of France and deported thousands of Jews and others who had taken refuge in the southeastern departments.

In January 1943 the Vichy regime set up the *milice* (militia), formed from Joseph Darnard's Service d'Ordre Légionnaire, the Veterans Legion. The *milice* was a paramilitary organization of volunteer toughs and fanatics recruited to stamp out the resistance. It was the most hated of all police forces because the men were French and worked in their home areas. They were a special threat to resisters because of their familiarity with the local community.[33]

Despite the numerous police and security forces in France and despite the German warnings against those opposing the military occupation, the resistance gradually became more visible. The "V for Victory" was chalked on sidewalks and buildings. French and British prisoners of war disappeared from camps; leaflets and newspapers appeared that blamed the Germans for many things, including the food shortages. On November 11, 1940, the anniversary of the armistice of 1918, several thousand Parisian students left their lycées and the university in the first sizable demonstration against the Germans. Assembled at the Arc de Triomphe to lay flowers at the tomb of the Unknown Soldier, they began to sing the "Marseillaise." Shots rang out and German soldiers charged the crowd, beating the students with rifle butts. More than 100 students, many of them women, were arrested, and the university was forbidden to hold classes for the remainder of the semester.

After the defeat of their armies, the British immediately became involved with resisters in France. British intelligence services had been smashed by the rapid German invasion of France, and they desperately needed information to prevent the Nazis from using France as a springboard for the invasion of England.

The British secret intelligence service was known by its initials as SIS or MI 6. Headed by Stewart Menzies, its first move was to set up new contacts and groups in France. For the French the most important man in the organization was Col. Claude Dansey, Menzies' assistant chief for operations, an impatient man who opposed letting women assume positions of leadership.[34] Under Dansey was Comdr. Kenneth Cohen, the head of the French section of MI 6, who had direct responsibility for encouraging and working with the groups in France that reported to MI 6. One of the most successful of these was the Alliance network of Marie Madeleine Fourcade.

In 1939 the British created a new intelligence organization called MI 9. Its functions included facilitating the escape of British prisoners of war, aiding the return to England of those who evaded capture in enemy-occupied territory, and interrogating the men who reached Britain. One of the escape lines given assistance by MI 9 was Comet, led by Andrée de Jongh.[35]

A third important British organization that worked with the resistance in France was the Special Operations Executive (SOE), which was independent of MI 6 and MI 9. An "irregular organization," it was instructed by Prime Minister Churchill in July 1940 "to set Europe ablaze" by encouraging revolt among the oppressed peoples under the Nazi heel. More specifically, SOE had two functions: to instigate sabotage against the enemy and to prepare secret armies to join in the liberation of their countries. In carrying out its mission SOE sent thousands of containers of arms, ammunition, and explosives by parachute drop into France.[36]

Since no one knew how much support de Gaulle had in France in the summer of 1940, SOE set up a French section called F to operate independently of the Free French in London. The British were willing to work with anyone in France who wanted to break the German stranglehold on the country, and did not want to be limited to Gaullists. Early in 1941, however, SOE became impressed with the support for de Gaulle in France, and in the spring set up a new section, RF, to work with the Free French. Its primary task was to encourage and support a unified resistance movement and a secret army in France. Not surprisingly, a virulent rivalry developed between the F and RF sections.[37]

SOE also had a West European escape section, DF. Its major responsibility was to run escape lines, some across France to the coast of Brittany and others to Spain. One of its most successful lines was Var, which transported 70 evaders and agents across the Channel to and from Brittany.[38]

Women played important roles in the various sections of SOE. Unlike the older services, this new and unorthodox organization was not bound by traditions about suitable tasks for women. It employed women not only because of the shortage of qualified men, but also because its staff saw the special advantages women could offer. Women were therefore trained in intelligence, radio communications, sabotage, paramilitary activities, and parachute jumping. Many served in England as staff officers, radio operators, and code clerks, and 39 were sent as agents to France.[39] Twelve of these were executed in German prisons or concentration camps, and one died of meningitis in the field.[40]

Free French groups were active as well. Two of these were the Deuxième Bureau (intelligence) and the Troisième Bureau (operations) of de Gaulle's headquarters, both assigned at first to Capt. André Dewavrin. The immediate task of the Deuxième Bureau was to provide the British with detailed information about German military preparations to invade England. By 1942 the two sections were combined into one London-based organization called the Bureau Central de Renseignements et d'Action (BCRA), the Central Bureau of Intelligence and Action. Dewavrin, who took the name of the metro station Passy as his pseudonym, continued as chief of the entire organization, which had its headquarters at 10 Duke Street. The intelligence section was then headed by André Manuel. It maintained liaison with the British MI 6; the operations section, concerned with sabotage and military actions, had close ties with the RF section of SOE, which supplied Gaullist networks and groups in France.[41]

Dewavrin also set up an evasion section in response to a request from MI 9. Additional escape lines were needed to rescue Allied aviators shot down over France. Dewavrin's first line, Brandy, was one of a family of Gaullist networks that took the name of French wines or liqueurs.[42]

In 1943 General de Gaulle moved his headquarters to Algiers, where he served first as co-president with Gen. Henri Giraud, and then, after a political struggle, as sole president of the new French Committee of National Liberation (CFLN).[43] Dewavrin's position was now changed. Jacques Soustelle became head in Algiers of de Gaulle's Secret Service, Direction Générale des Services Spéciaux (DGSS), with Dewavrin as his technical director. Continuity was maintained in London by the section under Manuel, the Bureau of Research and Action (BRAL), which continued to work with the RF section of SOE.[44]

Relations between the British RF section and the French BCRA were close but often strained. The British controlled the aircraft for parachute and pickup operations, the arms for sabotage actions, and radio communications; and this gave them a dominant position. There was uneasy cooperation between RF and BCRA but de Gaulle and Dewavrin deeply resented the existence of F section, believing it was a subversive rival to BCRA in France.[45]

Since BCRA was as unorthodox as SOE, it also broke tradition about the roles of women, but at a slower pace. Women served as couriers, radio operators, code clerks, and sabotage instructors. In 1944 BCRA sent 11 women agents to France, most of them by parachute. All of them survived.[46]

In contrast with Great Britain, the United States government did not become involved in the French resistance until after the Japanese attack on Pearl Harbor on December 7, 1941. When World War II began on September 1, 1939, the United States had no central intelligence organization. There was a feeling that spying was a dirty business and that gentlemen did not engage in such activities. President Franklin Roosevelt, however, realized that good intelligence was essential to sound policy, particularly regarding the war in Europe. In June 1941 he appointed a Republican Wall Street lawyer, William J. (Wild Bill) Donovan, a hero of World War I, as coordinator of information. Since Donovan believed that the United States faced a dangerous threat from the Nazis, he moved quickly to set up intelligence, special operations, counterespionage, and propaganda activities under COI.

One month before the Japanese bombed Pearl Harbor, COI set up its first overseas mission headquarters in London. Its primary purpose was to establish liaison with its British and French counterparts. In June 1942, COI became the more familiar Office of Strategic Services (OSS). As head of OSS, Donovan controlled both the intelligence and the special operations services. His Secret Intelligence section (SI) worked with MI 6 and with Dewavrin of BCRA, while the Special Operations section (SO) worked with SOE. This section concentrated on training and infiltrating sabotage teams into enemy-occupied territory.[47]

At the same time that Donovan was setting up OSS, the U.S. Army was establishing a group to work with the British MI 9. Lt. Col. W. Stull Holt, an academic historian and an Eighth Air Force intelligence officer in England, had been impressed by the early success of the British unit; and through his initiative an American P/W (prisoner of war) section was activated under his command in June 1942 and installed in Beaconsfield, the British escape and evasion center just west of London. The following February it became the P/W and X Detachment of G-2 (army intelligence) in Europe, and its X section was the American equivalent of MI 9. Its responsibilities remained the same, and included the briefing of American combat personnel about escape and evasion techniques, and the interrogation of American soldiers who had made their way back to Britain. As the escape chapters of this book will show, the interrogation reports based on these interviews are rich sources of information about what women were doing to help Allied military personnel escape from France.[48]

Since the United States was a latecomer to the European war, the inexperienced Americans learned from their British counterparts and OSS agents played the role of junior partners to MI 6 and SOE through 1943. When the Allies gained control of French North Africa in November 1942, OSS set up a headquarters in Algiers. The French desk of its intelligence section sent agents to France to obtain information about German defenses and military forces in the south of France. French and American women helped in this operation.

In preparation for D Day the activities of SOE and the Operations section (OS) of OSS were integrated in January 1944.[49] Four months later SOE/OSS was given the cover name Special Force Headquarters (SFHQ). In Algiers, in keeping with the new coordination, British SOE personnel and Americans from OSS formed the Special Projects Operations Center (SPOC). The French also became part of SPOC, and some Frenchwomen were parachuted into southern France to serve as couriers.[50] The purpose of SPOC was to support the French resistance in preparation for the American-

French invasion of southern France originally scheduled to coincide with the Allied invasion of Normandy. Because of the shortage of landing craft and the prior claims of the Italian campaign, the invasion did not take place until August 15, 1944.[51]

As soon as the Allies landed in Normandy on D Day, OSS set up teams that moved with several Allied armies. When Paris was liberated, a forward headquarters was established there that soon had contact with outposts at Lyon, Dijon, Toulouse, Marseille, Nice, and Annemasse. OSS personnel continued to provide military intelligence for the advancing armies and to arm French guerrilla groups, called the maquis, that were harassing and fighting the Germans. Beginning in January 1944, the U.S. Army Air Force (USAAF) dropped thousands of containers of weapons, ammunition, and explosives by parachute to the maquis, and the number was sharply increased after D Day.[52]

The British and Americans also contributed large sums of money to help finance the resistance. F section of SOE, for example, provided £2 million to its agents in France, some of which was obtained locally by loans from sympathetic businessmen. At the same time the British provided funds for BCRA, and from November 1943 to July 1944 RF section of SOE sent 1.33 billion francs either by agents or by parachute drops. Unfortunately some of this money did not reach the resistance because it was dropped to the wrong area or seized by the Germans.[53]

OSS also sent funds to France. The money was first dispatched from neutral Switzerland, where Allen W. Dulles served as chief of OSS in Bern under the transparent cover of "special assistant to the United States minister." Dulles sent money to Henri Frenay, chief of Combat, the largest resistance organization in the south of France, in exchange for copies of the intelligence reports that Frenay was sending to BCRA. Frenay believed that he needed more money to run Combat than he received from BCRA.[54] OSS also contributed money to other groups, including the numerous networks that its agents organized in France.[55]

As will be seen in the course of this book, the operation of underground organizations was costly. One of the big items was expense money for most of the full- and part-time workers. Those who served as organizers, couriers, guides, and liaison agents were usually compensated for their travel expenses: railroad tickets; meals in black market restaurants, which did not require ration tickets; and lodging in hotels or safehouses, where the hostess had to provide black market food purchased at exorbitant prices. Escape lines also paid the travel expenses of Allied aviators who were escorted across France to Brittany, or over the Pyrenees, where Basque guides charged heavy fees to lead them into Spain.

Thanks to the sheer determination of its members, the French resistance by 1944 had grown into a vast and highly complex structure. The country had been blanketed by more than 177 networks and subnetworks, and by 41 diversified resistance movements.[56] Together these underground workers sent reams of military intelligence to London, published several hundred clandestine newspapers with a total circulation of 2 million, helped 5,000 Allied airmen to escape from France, and furnished about 200,000 guerrilla soldiers to take part in the liberation of the country. In all of these activities, women played important roles. Though they fought without uniforms, they contributed significantly to the victory against the Germans.

What motivated these women to take the grave risk of standing up to the Germans by violating the armistice terms and by ignoring the decrees against the resistance? For many fiercely patriotic Frenchwomen the presence of any foreign troops in France would have been a sufficient motive to resist, but the fascist ideology was especially offensive to people like Yvonne Oddon and her associates at the Musée de l'Homme, who were fervently anti-Nazi. Many women remembered that German armies had destroyed their family homes or those of relatives in World War I, or even in the Franco-Prussian War of 1870. Since childhood they had heard the stories of German cruelties. Thousands of women in France had already either lost their husbands in the recent fighting or learned that their husbands, sons, or other relatives were prisoners of war. They had every reason to oppose the invaders.

Who were these women who joined the resistance in France? What were their social positions, their political and religious views? Were they all French? Women of all social classes were found in the resistance: aristocrats and peasants, middle-class housewives, and professionals like Lucie Aubrac, a teacher, and Yvonne Oddon, a librarian. The fact that so many and such diverse groups were represented in the ranks gave the resistance movement a wealth of resources for gathering and dispatching intelligence, helping to organize escapes, and sabotaging the enemy's operations.

Contrary to a common belief, women in the resistance were not all single and young. Thousands were married and mothers of families. Many had husbands who were prisoners of war. Others were divorced or widowed. All ages were represented: there were women in their seventies as well as teenagers.

Their political views, like their ages and social statuses, varied widely. Between the conservatives from aristocratic and military backgrounds and the Communist intellectuals and workers were women of all political leanings, including many with no political interests because they had not been enfranchised after World War I like women in many other countries. The Musée de l'Homme network included conservatives as well as left socialists.[57] In the escape line Shelburne, a conservative countess, although outnumbered by colleagues of the center and left, helped downed Allied airmen escape from France.[58]

In the Front National (FN) led by Communists, not only Communist women participated. After the Nazis violated the German-Soviet nonaggression pact of August 1939 and invaded the Soviet Union in June 1941, the

Communist Party abandoned its earlier opposition to the "imperialist war."
It set up a broad resistance movement encompassing people of political parties from the Communist to the conservative. Madeleine Braun, a leader of
the FN, explained that non-Communists should be part of the FN because
they all had the same goal: "To fight against the Germans and to liberate
France. After that they would see."[59]

Although France is a predominantly Roman Catholic country, both
Protestants and Jews played important roles in the resistance. Yvonne Oddon
and Elisabeth Dussauze, for example, were Protestants; Annie Kriegel, a
courier with some paramilitary groups, was one of many Jews in the resistance. The Protestants, being a small minority (1 percent of the population), had a history of "resistance" to the central government. The anti-Semitic
decrees of the German and Vichy governments gave the Jews a special motive
for resisting, even though arrest would place them in double jeopardy.

Not only were many social classes, political parties, and religions represented by the women in the resistance, but the movement embraced nationals
of different countries. Among those aiding the Frenchwomen in the resistance
were British, Belgian, and American women, as well as White Russian, Polish,
and German refugees.

During the war most women did not take into account their many differences. They were too busy dodging the police and carrying out their assign-
ments. Genevieve Soulié, who was in charge of providing lodging in Paris for
downed Allied airmen for the escape line Burgundy, summed it up this way: "In
our network there were Catholics, atheists, Protestants, Jews, and people of different political parties and social classes. Our view was that we were still at war
against the enemy occupying our country, and that was the important thing."[60]

Notes

1. This was 13 days after the Dutch had been crushed by the Nazi steamroller.
2. Henri Michel, *The Second World War*, pp. 122–23.
3. Charles de Gaulle, *The Complete War Memoirs*, pp. 59–68.
4. Ibid., p. 77.
5. Henri Philippe Pétain, *Actes et écrits*, pp. 448–49.
6. Marie Madeleine Fourcade, *Noah's Ark*, p. 22.
7. Brigitte Robert Muller, interview, Ann Arbor, MI, April 1976.
8. Hitler insisted that the French sign a companion armistice agreement with
the Italians. English text of the German-French and the Italian-French armistice
agreements is in *New York Times*, June 26, 1940.
9. The number of men echoed the restriction placed on the German army in
the Versailles Treaty of 1919, as did a requirement to pay occupation costs.
10. Robert O. Paxton, *Vichy France*, pp. 56–57, 87.

11. Not all members of Parliament were present. On June 21, 29 deputies and a senator had sailed to North Africa on the *Massilia* in an attempt to move the government there. They had been detained by Pétain's government and called "cowardly" for leaving metropolitan France. The 70-odd Communist members had been expelled from the Chamber of Deputies after the party had denounced the war against Hitler as an imperialist war of no concern to the workers. Ibid., pp. 29–32, 39.

12. Radio addresses of June 17 and 20, 1940, in Pétain, *Actes*, pp. 448–50.

13. Mme Suzanne Borel Bidault, interview, Paris, June 1974, and her *Souvenirs de guerre et d'occupation*, p. 91. As a civil servant in Vichy she helped an intelligence chief send information to England via the diplomatic pouch to Portugal. She also assisted patriots in escaping from France. Paul Paillole, *Services spéciaux 1935–1945*, p. 266. She married the prominent resister Georges Bidault after the war.

14. De Gaulle, *Memoirs*, pp. 27, 44, 67, 71.

15. Ibid., pp. 74–77.

16. Ibid., p. 80.

17. Ibid., pp. 83–84.

18. Henri Michel, *Bibliographie critique de la résistance*, p. 9.

19. De Gaulle, *Memoirs*, pp. 85, 94.

20. Germaine Tillion, letter to author, February 15, 1980.

21. Tillion, "Précis historique sur le réseau Hauet-Vildé," p. 4, Musée de l'Homme Collection, Ellen Clarke Bertrand Library, Bucknell University, Lewisburg, PA.

22. Martin Blumenson, *The Vildé Affair*, p. 64.

23. Tillion, "Précis historique," pp. 1–4.

24. Yvonne Oddon, "Rapport sur mon activité de résistance," p. 1, Musée de l'Homme Collection, Bucknell University.

25. Ibid., pp. 1–2. The group at the Musée de l'Homme had contacts with the American embassy, an intelligence group, and a writer's group.

26. Ibid., p. 8.

27. Tillion, "Précis historique," p. 5, and letter to author, February 15, 1980. Hauet was soon released from prison because of his advanced age and because de La Rochère assumed all responsibility for their intelligence activity.

28. Ibid.

29. Tillion, letter to author, October 19, 1979.

30. Confédération Nationale de Combattants Volontaires de la Résistance, "Echo de la Résistance," no. 100, 1964.

31. Hugo Bleicher, *Colonel Henri's Story*, p. 45; Paillole, pp. 64–66.

32. In the spring of 1944, Himmler, following a series of German military defeats, won the bitter internal struggle with Canaris and took over the Abwehr.

33. M. R. D. Foot, *SOE in France*, p. 120.

34. M. R. D. Foot and J. M. Langley, *MI 9*, p. 80.

35. Ibid., pp. 34–35.

36. Foot, *SOE*, pp. 20, 474.

37. Ibid., p. 21.

38. Ibid., p. 69.

39. See material on the French BCRA, below.

40. Foot, *SOE*, pp. 46–48, 465–69.

41. André Dewavrin [Colonel Passy], *2ᵉ bureau, Londres*, p. 166; and *10 Duke Street, Londres*, pp. 29–32, 45.

42. Dewavrin, *10 Duke Street*, p. 33.

43. President Roosevelt, suspicious of General de Gaulle's aims, supported General Giraud.

44. Foot, *SOE*, pp. 22–23. To avoid confusion, I will refer to de Gaulle's secret services as BCRA. Following the liberation, DGSS was replaced by the Direction Général d'Etudes et Recherches (DGER), which had an evasion section.

45. Eric Piquet-Wicks, *Four in the Shadows*, pp. 22–30; Henri Michel, *Histoire de la résistance en France*, p. 80; Dewavrin, *10 Duke Street*, pp. 165–68.

46. Jeanne Bohec, *La plastiqueuse à bicyclette*, pp. 23, 69–73, 100; Foot, *SOE*, p. 469.

47. Ray S. Cline, *Secrets, Spies, and Scholars*, pp. 59, 65; Dewavrin, *10 Duke Street*, pp. 144–46.

48. In early May 1945, the work of the Awards Section of P/W and X Detachment was continued under the name of 6801 MIS-X Detachment. RG 332, ETO, MIS, MIS-X Section, General Correspondence 1942–47, File 314.7, "History of 6801 MIS-X Detachment"; RG 407, Records of the Adjutant General's Office, "Directive of Secretary of War," WD October 6, 1942, File 383.6, vol. 1.

49. U.S. War Department, Strategic Services Unit, History Project, *War Report of the OSS*, 2:191.

50. Mary Eddy Furman, interview, Washington, D.C., February 1980.

51. RG 165, Records of the War Department General and Special Staffs, Gen. Henry Maitland Wilson, "The Invasion of Southern France," OPD 319.1, TS-Opr, Case no. 33.

52. W. F. Craven and J. L. Cate, eds., *The Army Air Forces in World War II*, 3:503–05; Foot, *SOE*, pp. 474–75; Marcel Vigneras, *Rearming the French*, p. 305.

53. Foot, *SOE*, pp. 470–74.

54. Henri Frenay, *The Night Will End*, pp. 102, 263–64.

55. For information on OSS/Bern networks, see U.S. War Department, *War Report of the OSS*, 2:181.

56. "Liste des réseaux et des mouvements," Ministry of Defense (Paris), Office of Veterans, manuscript list. In the course of the war there were more networks, but because of the diligence of German police agencies, many were destroyed without trace. F section of SOE had a total of 93 networks, 43 of which were extinct by the time France was liberated. Foot, *SOE*, pp. 145–46.

57. Tillion, "Première résistance en zone occupé," *Revue d'histoire de la deuxième guerre mondiale*, April 1958, p. 7.

58. Genevieve de Poulpiquet, interview, Paris, October 1976.

59. Madeleine Braun, interview, Paris, October 1976.

60. Genevieve Soulié Camus, interview, Paris, October 1976. After the liberation, social and political differences reappeared in many organizations.

II WOMEN TO THE RESCUE— ESCAPE LINES

2 NOTABLE CHIEFS

When the German Panzer divisions broke through the French defenses and dashed to the English Channel in May 1940, they trapped French and British forces, which withdrew to Dunkerque. More then 338,000 Allied troops were rescued in an improvised sea operation, but many others were left behind. Forty thousand French troops were taken prisoner by the Germans, while several thousand soldiers of the British Expeditionary Force either avoided capture by hiding on farms and in towns or, like many French soldiers, escaped from temporary prisoner of war enclosures and hospitals.[1]

The German victory created an immediate need for organized operations that would help Allied soldiers and sympathizers escape to Britain. The earliest efforts by patriots wanting to do something for the Allies were feeding, sheltering, and transporting the fugitives they met more or less accidentally. For example, the first escape routes were established by Breton fishermen, who dodged German patrol boats in the Channel while taking volunteers to England to fight for the Free French. Eventually, with the assistance of British and Free French organizations, such as MI 9 and BCRA, such impromptu aid by ordinary people gradually developed into a complex structure of escape lines involving about 100,000 resisters, many of whom were women. During the course of the war they helped almost 2,000 British and Commonwealth airmen and 3,000 American fliers to escape from northwest Europe, primarily France.[2]

Assisting in the return of Allied airmen shot down over occupied territory was an especially important service, since the British suffered from a desperate shortage of fighter and bomber pilots and crewmen, and it took time and money to train them: £15,000 for a fighter pilot and £23,000 for the seven-man crew of a Lancaster bomber.[3]

When the Germans increased their coastal surveillance in order to halt further escapes by sea, land routes were organized. Some extended more than 700 miles from Brussels across occupied France to Spain. Once the soldiers arrived in Spain, they had to avoid arrest by the police, and those who succeeded were guided to British consulates that arranged their transportation to Gibraltar. The unlucky ones who were imprisoned had to wait several months before the British or American consular services could arrange their release.

Other escape lines crossed the demarcation line, the formidable barrier that separated German-occupied northern France from the unoccupied zone of the Vichy government. Headquarters for these lines were set up in cities such as Marseille, from which the soldiers were passed westward along the coast to Perpignan and the Pyrenees. Sometimes the men were evacuated by British boats at night, particularly from Mediterranean beaches such as Canet Plage near Perpignan. Later in the war Allied airmen were picked up from the northern coast of Brittany by British gunboats.

Thousands of women responded to the challenge of helping stranded Allied soldiers, and many became leaders in the escape organizations. Four women headed large escape organizations: the lines known as Comet, Françoise, Marie Claire, and Marie Odile. At least ten women were chiefs of smaller lines, and many were subchiefs or heads of regional sectors. Other women also are known to have exercised leadership in these organizations.

In addition to being leaders of escape lines, women made up a significant proportion of the membership ranks. According to Georges Broussine, chief of Burgundy, about 40 percent of the helpers in his line were women. In the Comet organization, which had members in Belgium and France, some 65 to 70 percent were women. Lists of those who were singled out for postwar awards indicate that 36 percent of the recipients in the Marie Odile line, 20 percent in the Françoise line, and 35 percent in Brandy were women. These lists, however, do not reveal the total number of people associated with the organizations because the names of those who performed only infrequent service do not appear.

The Comet line grew out of a young Belgian woman's conviction that the principal effort to assist Allied soldiers should be directed toward arranging their escape to England as rapidly as possible. In this way the Belgians could help to reduce the critical British need for airmen and lessen the danger that the patriots who gave them shelter would be arrested by the Germans. Originally called the Dédée line after its founder, Andrée (Dédée) de Jongh, it later acquired the name Postman because she referred to the escaping airmen as "packages" and her code name among the British was Postman. Later Dédée named the line Comet because it returned the airmen so quickly to their bases in Britain.

This 24-year-old Belgian was the younger daughter of Frédéric de Jongh, the headmaster of a primary school in Schaerbeek, an industrial section on

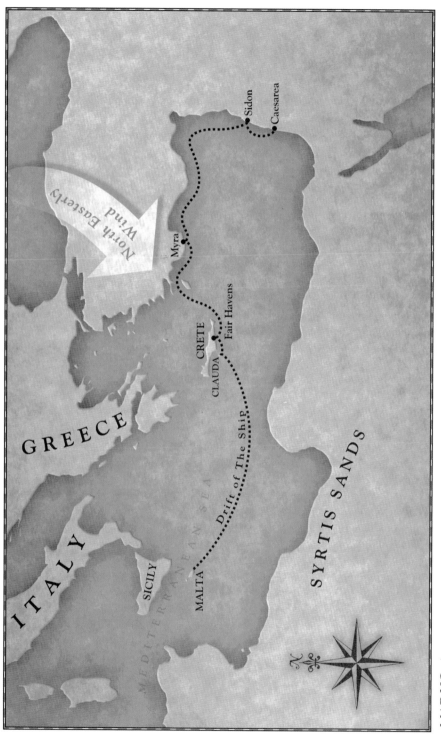

MAP NO. 1

Inset map detail shown on MAP NO. 3

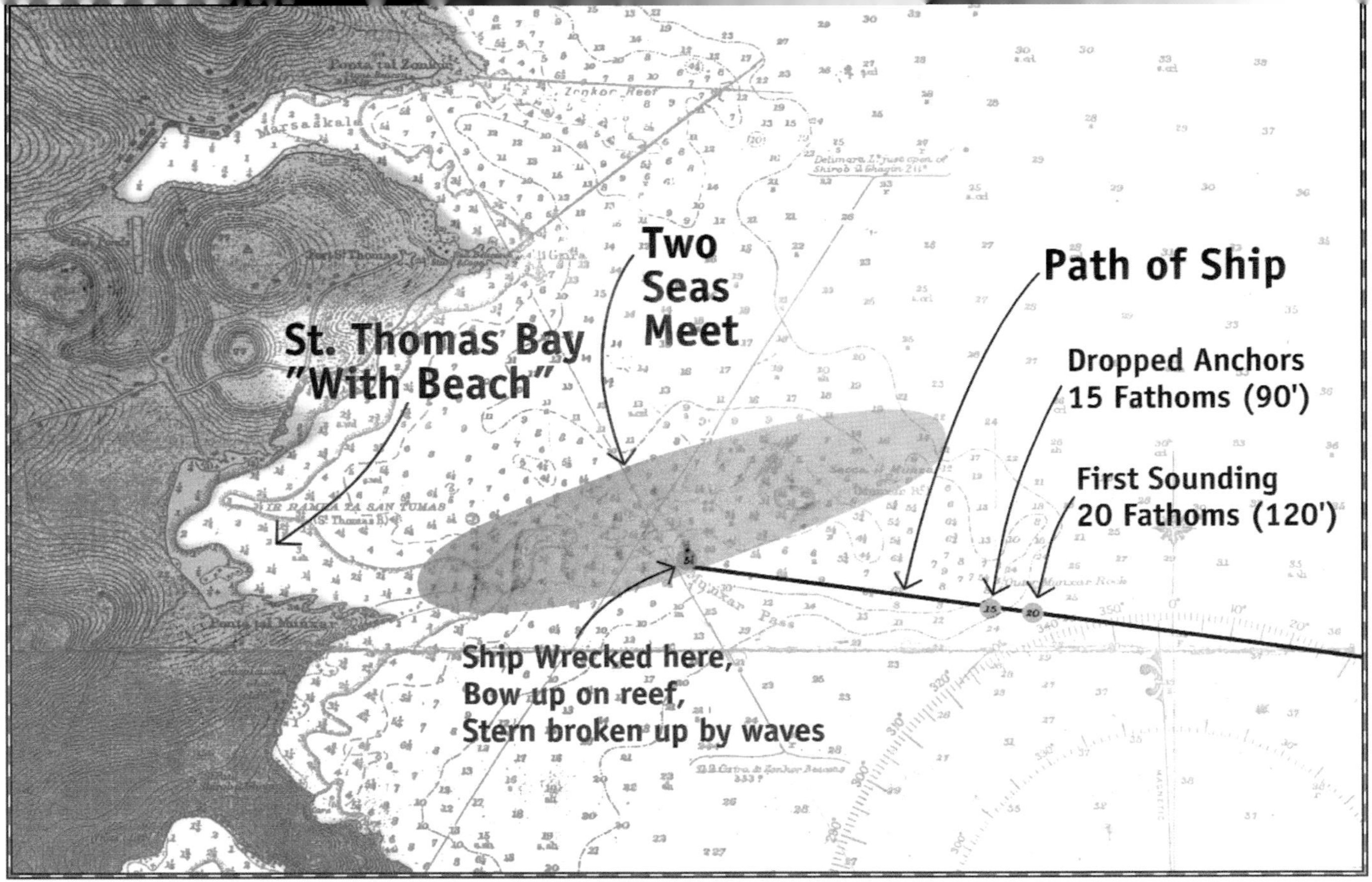

Path of Ship

Dropped Anchors
15 Fathoms (90')

First Sounding
20 Fathoms (120')

Two
Seas
Meet

St. Thomas Bay
"With Beach"

Ship Wrecked here,
Bow up on reef,
Stern broken up by waves

MAP NO. 3

3

One of the first dive canisters used by early divers on Malta

Wilfred Perotta (right) with Tony Micallef Borg Tony was renowned as a great diver on Malta and involved with bringing three of the anchors from the Munxar Reef

Wilfred Perotta (left) with unknown dive companion displaying a pole of grouper from the old days of spear fishermen. Circa 1960s

Author Robert Cornuke (left), Professor Bonanno, and Charles Grech kneel behind the anchor found by Tony and Charles in the early 70s on the Munxar Reef.

Anchor stock found by Ray and Tony in the early 70s on the Munxar Reef.

Lead dive weight from melted anchor stock found by Tony and Ray on the Munxar Reef in the early 70s. (Note the 'MT' chiseled on the face of the dive weight.)

Anchor stock found by "Mario" in the late 60s on the Munxar Reef.

6

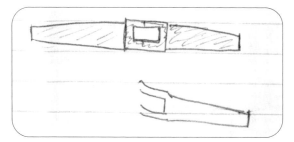

The hand sketch of cut/melted anchor by witness
Charlie Vella.

Model of an ancient
Roman/Alexandrian anchor.
The wood would have decayed rapidly
in the sea, but the lead cross piece
known as the anchor stock would last
indefinitely on the ocean floor.

Picture of Marsaxlokk Bay with traditional Maltese fishing boats called Luzzu.

Left to right: Angela Phillips, Dr. Mark Phillips, Dave Ladell, Jean Francois La'Archevec

Cliffs just north of St. Thomas Bay.

Bob Cornuke (left) with Jim Fitzgerald on a sandy beach of St. Thomas Bay. (Author believes this is the beach where St. Paul and surviving shipmates swam to shore following the shipwreck.)

This photo was taken during mild storm surf on the Munxar Reef "where two seas meet."

(Note: the currents come together on the reef from different directions.)

A reenactment of how Tony and Ray lifted the anchors from the sea using barrels filled with air.

St. Paul's Island, the island of legend where many say St. Paul's ship came to rest (the Bible says the ship of Paul was stuck on a **reef**). The geographical features found on St. Paul's Island do not match with the Biblical narrative.

BASE research team left to right: Jim Fitzgerald, Bryan Boorujy, Jerry Nordskog, Gail Nordskog, Jay Fitzgerald, Bob Cornuke, Yvonne Miles, Edgar Miles, David Stotts, Jeremy Miles (in back)

Wilfred Perotta with Ray Ardizzone holding the first dive tanks used in Malta.

12

Ray Ciancio, the protégé of Tony. When he was 14 years old he witnessed the discovery of two anchors found on the Munxar Reef.

Robert Cornuke (in the white shirt) in Afghanistan with pushtun body guards.

Author with Major Manuel Mallia inputting data into the computer to analyze direction of the drift of Paul's ship from Crete to Malta.

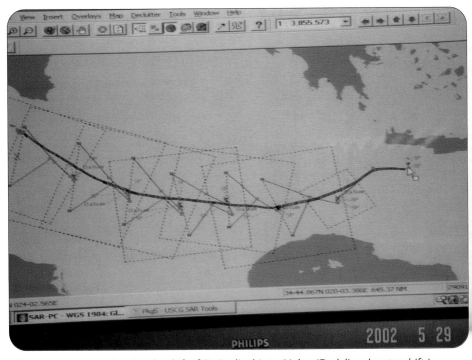

Computer program showing the drift of St. Paul's ship to Malta. (Dark line denotes drift.)

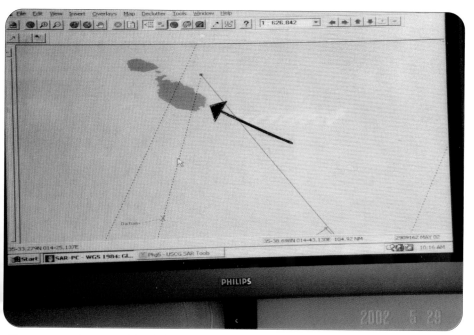

The computer determined the drift of Paul's ship coming from the south, encountering the island of Malta on the Southeast coast in the area of St. Thomas Bay.

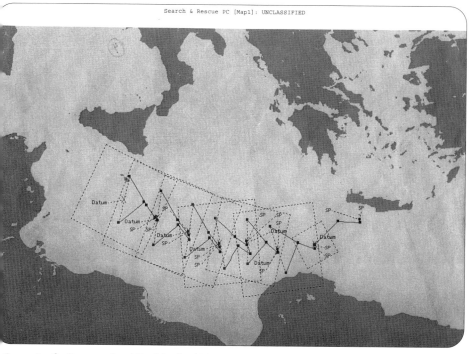

Computer findings on the drift of Paul's ship.

Lead sounding weight—a device used on ancient Roman vessels. The weight was tied to a rope and dropped into the sea to determine sea depth.

Just north of St. Thomas Bay, a freighter lies victim of a 'gregale' storm. The waves are crashing over 80 feet h

Khyber Pass, across which invading armies have traveled for thousands of years. Upon arriving at the border crossing in Afghanistan, we were greeted by thousands of people walking, driving, limping on crutches, and being carried on litters—all desperately trying to escape Afghanistan. Swarms of disabled and homeless men, women, and children congregated at the border crossing, staring helplessly through barbed wire gates through which they would never be allowed to pass.

AFGHANISTAN—DECEMBER 2001

Descending from the Khyber Pass, we drove alongside a meandering camel caravan and entered the northeastern frontier of Afghanistan. Across this vast no-man's-land of lawless disorder, grief and graves were all that remained. Everyone, it seemed, carried some kind of a rifle, pistol, or grenade launcher. Small boys wore ammunition belts proudly strapped to their chests, and we could sense an almost overpowering cloud of oppression—it filled the air, clung to one's skin. Generations of death and war had choked all joy and hope from these people. Children played among the carcasses of tanks and armored vehicles that littered the landscape, and the barren, dust-caked hillsides lay pocked with moonlike craters, like a scene from Hades.

Within a few hours we had reached Jalalabad, which would serve as our home base during our stay. The smoky, dust-shrouded sunset brought a gloomy end to another day of historic suffering in Afghanistan. We spent the night in a mud-walled compound. Armed civilian soldiers passed by my window every few minutes, their slow-moving forms casting eerie shadows from the pale moonlight. My bed consisted of a blanket spread over a mat on the floor. A Kalashnikov AK-47 machine gun had been "lovingly" placed on my pillow, a gift from my Pushtun host.

The Pushtuns are mountain people, vast in number, comprising a major portion of Afghanistan's population. Since there are over sixty different tribes in the country, the Pushtuns are in constant struggle with one another for land and power; feuds between families are often passed down from generation to generation. Unwritten codes rule tribal conduct and include, among a host of bizarre social rituals, the protection of guests—and I was a guest of a Pushtun tribal leader named Nastrula.

Nastrula was a friend of Joe Ritchie, whose self-appointed mission was simply to help his people, by whatever means possible. He had worked on numerous relief-aid projects, some of which involved repairing parks and damaged irrigation systems traditionally used for the underground poppy trade. In Afghanistan, growing poppies had fueled a huge heroin trade, diverting critical agricultural irrigation and manpower from other, food producing crops. Joe was committed to helping Nastrula implement some sort of reform and redirection of these illicit activities toward "life-giving" agricultural projects. It was a terribly risky outreach, but I was impressed to see that Nastrula and Joe had made important inroads to help stem the region's deadly preoccupation.

The next day I would be traveling to Kabul to try and find the prison and the place where Dayna and Heather had left their journals. Nastrula assigned me two guards with machine guns and a van and driver for the long, bone-jarring journey. Before I left on my trip to Kabul, however, a war correspondent from the *Sunday Times of London* warned me that people were being attacked on the road to Kabul all the time.

"If you go to Kabul," he cautioned, "take no less that three trucks of armed guards."

When I told him I was going with only two guards and a van, he shrugged. "Well, then, you'll be my next story for the *Times.*"

It took five hot, jarring hours traveling through a swirling dust storm to reach the city of Kabul. More so than anywhere else we'd visited in Afghanistan, the landscape here was dominated by the remnants of war: Tanks, destroyed buildings, bombed-out neighborhoods filled the horizon as far as we could see. It was a scene that previously I had witnessed only on CNN; now I was now driving through the middle of it.

Night was falling by the time I arrived at the Kabul prison that had served as Heather and Dayna's temporary jail. It was really a "women's reform school" that had been used by the Taliban as a prison for women who were disobedient to their husbands, their fathers, or their faith. As Dayna and Heather had discovered, the slightest offense would land a woman in this cruel compound. In Afghanistan women could be beaten for simply wearing nail polish and could not work outside the home unescorted by a male family member. And under Taliban rule, if a taxi driver so much as drove a woman alone, he could be severely beaten for the offense.

So far I had encountered no resistance from the locals, which seemed somewhat odd. The United States military was currently pulverizing this country, cleansing it from the Taliban pestilence, and one would think an American civilian would attract unwelcome attention. To this point in the journey we had been spared, but as I strolled toward the front of the prison, a machine-gun-carrying bearded man walked over to me and stood with his arms crossed.

He introduced himself as a Northern Alliance commander and barked, "It will be impossible for you to enter today."

"All I want to do is take some film of the prison," I said, holding up my video camera.

"No! Forbidden!"

I had been in these situations before and had learned a few tricks. From my jacket pocket I removed a new watch, purchased for $6.95 at a Wal-Mart in Colorado. I pressed a button on the side, a pale green glow illuminating the dial. I placed the watch respectfully in his hand and said, "This watch is my gift to you."

He took the watch, looked around, and whispered, "This prison is my gift to you."

Within minutes I was videotaping Heather and Dayna's prison cell—a small, dirty room located off of a courtyard that was barren and dusty but for a lone tree in the middle. Heather and Dayna had faxed me a map they had sketched of the prison, and as I surveyed the scene, I knew I had found the right place.

Heather and Dayna told me as a way of identifying their cell that a woman in their group had mixed fingernail polish with mud and painted animal figures on the walls. Since the Taliban forbade paintings of any kind, the pictures had been whitewashed over, though one rough drawing of an elephant remained on the back wall. (Heather later told me that someone else probably sketched the elephant drawing after their escape.) The only thing that remained in their cell area was a blue strip of cloth stretched across the room to serve as a clothesline. I pulled down the blue cloth, rolled it up, and placed it in my pocket. Heather had said that every evening hundreds of flies perched on this blue cloth, offering the women a little "entertainment" during their imprisonment.

The next day I videotaped the home where the missionaries had lived prior to their arrest. Another commander in Kabul told me that the journals of the American women had been burned, so by noon the next day I left Kabul to return to Jalalabad.

As I drove through the Kabul Pass toward Jalalabad, my driver and guards pointed out men with guns on a ridge on the canyon walls. They then directed my attention to large dried bloodstains spread across the ground. "This is where, just one month ago, robbers robbed and then killed four journalists," my driver said. Gazing at the bloodstained rocks, the driver motioned discreetly toward the men on the cliffs, heads wrapped in turbans, rifles in hand.

"Al-Qaida," he whispered. "It is very dangerous for us. We must go now."

PAUL'S ENDURANCE

The guns, the blood, the war, the maimed children, the insects, and the oppressing dust storms made for one of the most arduous trips I've ever been involved in. This was a foreboding land immersed in misery.

I thought, *How in the world did the apostle Paul do it?* Enduring year after years of lonely, dangerous travel into hostile, alien cities and lands. I had traveled a few thousand miles and had been away from home for two weeks, but it is estimated by some that Paul traveled over twenty thousand miles in his various journeys.[20] That's twenty thousand miles without planes, trains, or cars, every mile of it on foot, by hoofed transportation, or ancient ships. And, as he himself wrote,

> *...in labors more abundant, in stripes above measure,*
> *in prisons more frequently, in deaths often. From the*

149

Jews five times I received forty stripes minus one; three
times I was beaten with rods; once I was stoned; three
times I was shipwrecked; a night and a day I have been
in the deep; in journeys often, in perils of waters, in per-
ils of robbers, in perils of my own countrymen, in perils
of the Gentiles, in perils of the city, in perils in the sea,
in perils among false brethren; in weariness and toil, in
sleeplessness often, in hunger and thirst, in fastings
often, in cold and nakedness. (2 Corinthians 11:23–27)

Paul traveled thousands of miles, among warring tribal factions and dens of robbers. Through beatings, shipwrecks, and hardships, he traversed that brutal and unforgiving ancient world, enduring it all, every day, tirelessly spreading a message he knew to be true.

The man who once persecuted Christians was met on a roadway by his Lord and entrusted with a message that he would spread even in the face of death. He didn't stay in the confines of his protective group, but went out into a wild and dangerous world that wanted him dead.

Here in Afghanistan I could plainly see that, like Paul, Heather and Dayna had traveled a similar road. They had endured arrest, suffered persecution, and were even were spit on as they share their faith. There is always a price to pay when you take a stand for what you believe. Paul ultimately died for his allegiance. But, as that great apostle said, "For to me, to live is Christ, and to die is gain" (Philippians 1:21).

A person who converts from the Muslim to Christian faith in Afghanistan is considered dead by his or her family. He or she is severed from family ties, cut off socially. This social segregation for accepting an alternative to Islam prevents almost anyone from proclaiming a new faith of any kind. It's not surprising to me that today Afghanistan is estimated to be 99 percent Muslim.

Paul met with similar prospects in his efforts to share his faith. If someone from a Hebrew family accepted the Christian faith, that person was also considered dead by the family. But even in the face of constant persecution, Paul never stopped preaching the Word. He was relentless.

Traveling the dangerous back roads on our way back to Jalalabad, I couldn't help but think of Paul's commitment to his faith and his gutsy resolve. Feared, hated, beaten, robbed, spit on—nothing stopped him. In God's plan, nothing could.

ANCHORS OF HOPE

During my return flight to the United States, I mentally replayed my experiences in war-torn Afghanistan. I reached for my Bible to perhaps gain some perspective. I found myself journeying once again through the pages of Luke's narration and lingered over the words Paul penned from lonely outposts and prisons across the perilous ancient Mid-east. In my time on Malta, and now in the blood-soaked land of Afghanistan, I felt that I had met this man named Paul in a more personal way.

I discovered that this man who changed history's course was now changing mine.

The anchor I had touched on September 10, 2001, had suddenly become something more than mere lead. To me, the anchors had become a symbol of hope, a witness to one of the greatest stories ever told—of deliverance from death of those on Paul's ship who had lost all hope so long ago. As I stared out the window of the plane, my mind traveled back to the Munxar Reef and Malta's secretive fraternity of divers. If those anchors really were the anchors from Paul's ship, then those with no hope in their lives needed to know. With the death and devastation of Afghanistan now behind me, I felt more inspired than ever to continue the search. ⚓

Chapter Thirteen

THE MAN PAUL

he fondest memories I recall from my youth in Southern California are those when I was sitting with my grandmother on her plastic-covered sofa, having her read to me from books about far off places. Grandma was an immigrant from Russia, and when reading, she slowly enunciated each word because of her thick Slavic accent. Despite no formal education, she would walk to the library every week, check out three or more books, carry them home, and read each one. As I quietly sat there, I listened to her read on and on, intently watching while she slowly turned each page with her frail, silk-skinned hands. With a stack of books, Grandma could carry me away to distant, exotic lands, setting my sails for a life of travel and adventure.

As I reread many of the books of the New Testament that the apostle Paul wrote, I realized that no one has ever come close to the experiences of Paul when it came to travel and adventure. Not only had he traveled most of the known world during his time——enduring deprivation and suffering hardships that would have caused even the boldest explorers to quit, Paul amazingly counted those brutal trials and travels as both an honor and a privilege. He forged ahead through beatings, hunger, imprisonment, even shipwreck, until, as he said himself, "His very life had been poured out like a goblet of wine."

A CITIZEN OF ROME

The Rome of Paul's day had overcome its ancient beginnings as a poor, obscure, small city-state east of the bend of the Tiber River to become the world's most powerful empire. The Romans were disciplined, hard-working builders of magnificent cities and colossal monuments, and a succession of visionary emperors acted on their insatiable need for power. Rome's military leaders were cunning in battle and strategic in their political alliances.

From beyond Rome's far frontiers, kings and ambassadors brought opulent gifts and tributes to placate the empire. They knew that to be allied with Rome meant safety and protection. A friend of Rome enjoyed extensive personal rights and privileges. An enemy of Rome typically faced death and destruction.

Paul was born a Roman citizen in Tarsus and educated by the Rabbi Gamaliel in Jerusalem. Paul came to hate Christians and persecuted them with a peculiar drive and zeal. On one occasion he held the garments of a mob stoning a follower of Christ, named Stephen. Paul feared the new cult of "believers" that had multiplied so quickly around the teachings of the so-called heretic Jesus, who had so blasphemously proclaimed Himself to be the Son of God and had been put to death on a cross. Jesus had spoken out against the hypocrisy, lies, and legalism of the Jewish Pharisees—a privileged class of rabbis and priests (of whom Paul had sacrificed all to become a distinguished member). Paul, in turn, became a relentless, self-appointed pursuer of any and all who held to this Jesus' radical teachings, presiding over the deaths and imprisonment of scores of Christians and contributing in no small part to the scattering of the early church. Little did he know that life as he knew it was about to end. Paul was about to go from the hater to the hated, from the hunter to the hunted.

Most of us have heard of Paul's dramatic conversion experience since we were children in Sunday school: Paul, en route to Damascus to arrest more followers of "The Way," encountered a flashing light brighter than the sun and fell to the ground blinded. From within the light he heard the voice of Jesus, the Messiah of Israel, asking, "Why are you persecuting Me?"—a short sentence that marked the start of the incredible ministry of one of the New Testament's great apostles. Within a short time this ruthless persecutor of the church had undergone an amazing transformation that baffled his allies, confused his enemies, and ultimately, changed the world forever.

At first the Christians feared Paul, unable to believe that their former jailer now preached Jesus as *Messiah*. His old cronies, the Jewish Pharisees, stamped him as a lunatic traitor to their faith. Much like Paul had been only months before, they could not stomach the fact that an executed criminal named Jesus could have so many followers so many years after his execution. And, then, in the type of inexplicable turnabout that made their blood boil, Paul himself, their lead persecutor, had converted too. It certainly filled them with a disgust that, on a smaller scale, exceeded their hatred of the Romans, who still occupied their land. No one could have confronted the depths of their religious hypocrisy like this formerly high-ranking Jew now preaching the new religion of the man whom he talked about as being the "Son of God." Plainly put, Paul had committed national treason because of his new belief, and the Pharisees vowed to get rid of him.

Their first opportunity arrived when Paul entered the Temple in Jerusalem after having publicly fraternized with unclean Gentiles. Upon hearing that Paul had entered the Temple compound with his "filthy" friends in tow, the Pharisees quickly formed a mob and descended on the Temple complex. Once inside, the angry throng grabbed Paul and dragged him out of the compound, beating him with the intent to kill. As news of the riot reached the Roman commander, he went with a company of soldiers to the angry crowd.

After quieting the riot, the Romans guards bound Paul in chains and took him to the barracks. The commander of the Roman forces in Judea saw no reason for a trial for this Jewish troublemaker: A riot had started in the streets of Jerusalem and Paul was clearly to blame. He would be beaten until he confessed, or died.

A soldier stood near Paul and tensed his grip around the whip, a menacing ensemble of leather thongs interwoven with jagged bits of metal and bone. But before the centurion could administer this patently Roman form of justice, Paul lifted his bloody face and sternly inquired, "Is it lawful for you to scourge a man who is a Roman and uncondemned?"

The soldier's outstretched arm dropped to his side, his whip dangling in the dirt. The centurion immediately went to the commander and told him that the Jewish prisoner has just claimed to be a citizen of Rome; and with that, Paul's destiny changed.

(For a Jew in Roman Judea, it was nothing unusual to be dragged to jail, accused of being suspicious, and then beaten into submission. But to flog a *citizen* of Rome, especially without a trial or legal condemnation, was strictly forbidden.)

The commander quickly came to Paul and asked, "Are you a Roman citizen?"

"Yes," Paul replied.

Shocked, the commander probed further to see if his prisoner was simply a wealthy Jew who had bribed his way to a privileged position.

"With a large sum I obtained this citizenship," the Commander said. (Obviously he wasn't born a Roman citizen.) Paul replied, "I was *born* a citizen."

Alarmed at realizing that he had put a Roman citizen in chains, the commander contemplated his next move and ordered Paul to be untied. The next morning, hoping to clear up what had become a confusing mess, the commander ordered all the chief priests and their council to appear before him. Minutes later Paul stood before the crowd to give an account of himself. "Men and brethren," he began, "I have lived in all good conscious before God until this day."

Even this basic claim so incensed the high priest that he ordered Paul hit about the mouth. Spitting blood, Paul shot back at them, saying in essence, "You hit me without charge, you hypocrite. You sit and judge me, and you strike me without being charged, so you're the one who breaks the law."

By meeting's end, another furious mob had tried to wring Paul's neck, and once again the soldiers had to drag him to safety. Paul was later ordered to appear in Rome and would continue to contend with brazen threats against his life—in one case narrowly escaping a clandestine plot by forty men bound with an oath to neither eat nor drink until Paul was dead.

Ultimately, two hundred soldiers, seventy horsemen, and two hundred spearmen accompanied Paul on his way to Caesarea, illustrating just how great a sensation this story had become in the middle of the first-century Roman world. Paul was big news, already renowned among believers in that region—many of whom believed that even handkerchiefs and garments Paul touched would heal the sick. And now his peculiar fame had spread across the empire, triggering deep, passionate emotions in everyone who heard his story.

In Caesarea, Paul fell under the jurisdiction of Felix, a former slave himself, who rose (with the help of some strategic marriages) to become Governor of Judea. A greedy man, Felix let his famous prisoner sit in jail, hoping to collect a substantial bribe, with the result that Paul languished in a prison for two more years.

"YOU ALMOST PERSUADE ME TO BECOME A CHRISTIAN."

Paul's fate would veer toward the island of Malta when Felix was replaced as governor by a fellow named Festus. Confronted with the same politically risky mess that Felix had faced, Festus tried to make it easy on himself. He simply asked Paul if he would be willing to be tried in Jerusalem.

Paul refused and demanded to make his appeal directly to Caesar.

In those days, every citizen of the Roman Empire had the right to appeal to Rome, or "Caesar's judgment seat." In Paul's case, it presented a dangerous logistical dilemma, for the prisoner would have to be transported all the way back to the city of Rome, where he would then be held until his case could be heard in the high court. But Festus apparently saw it as an easy out, for after hearing Paul's abbreviated defense and appeal to Caesar, he readily replied, "You have appealed to Caesar? To Caesar you shall go."

Confined to prison while waiting at Caesarea for his transfer to Rome, Paul had a unique opportunity to speak directly with King Agrippa II, who visited Caesarea to welcome Festus to his new post. Agrippa II was the grandson of the infamous Herod the Great, who had tried to kill the infant Messiah by slaughtering all the male children less than two years of age in the districts of Bethlehem. Herod's grandson apparently shared the same arrogant disregard for the God of the Jews that had motivated his demented grandfather. One writer described the Herod family tree as "infested...murder, maneuvers for power, incest, and moral dissoluteness marked its many branches preceding and during the incarnate and risen ministry of Jesus Christ."[21]

Yet Agrippa II took an unexpected personal liking to Paul. Though Festus had no way of knowing that Rome's ruler in Judea would take an interest in this lowly Jewish prisoner, he explained the chain of events that led to Paul's arrest and imprisonment. Festus must have been stunned when Agrippa quickly called for an impromptu hearing. We can only imagine the tension that must have been hanging in the air as Festus set up the assembly and then watched Agrippa and Bernice glide through the standing crowd to their royally appointed thrones. The regal pair no doubt looked around the room until all was perfectly silent, and once all eyes were on them, they took their seats.

With a wave of his hand, Festus ordered the chained prisoner brought before the assembly, detailing the strange sequence of events that brought Paul to Festus's court. Agrippa turned toward Paul and said, "You are permitted to speak for yourself" (Acts 26:1).

Here again, Paul's audience with the king demonstrated the persuasive power of the gospel. Paul's speech played to Agrippa's prior knowledge of all things Jewish—so much so, in fact, that by the end of his oratory, Festus had no better response than to issue a feeble insult to Paul's intelligence: "Paul," he cried, "you are beside yourself! Much learning is driving you mad!"

The place undoubtedly erupted in laughter.

As the uproar subsided, Paul's response must have drawn a collective gasp from the crowd for its brashness in the face of Roman might: "I am not mad, most noble Festus," Paul replied calmly, "but speak the words of truth and reason." He then appealed to what he knew of Agrippa's expertise in the Hebrew Scriptures and challenged it directly. Paul—the lowly Jewish prisoner, bruised and scarred, disheveled, and probably sick from two years of prison—stood bound in chains in front of the highest authority in Judea, then spoke one of the most courageous lines in all of courtroom history.

"King Agrippa," he said, "do you believe the prophets? I know you do believe." Paul spoke these brazen words to the highest authority in Judea, challenging the spiritual accountability of the king himself. The audience could scarcely believe the gall of the accused.

Even two thousand years later, it strikes us as a brilliant, disarming question. For if Agrippa indeed professed to believe in the prophets, he undoubtedly knew that Jesus fulfilled, in detail, exactly what the prophets wrote about Messiah in the Hebrew Scriptures. It also meant that Paul was innocent and should be released. However, if Agrippa said he didn't believe the prophets, he would offend the Jewish leaders, who took the writings of the prophets as the very Word of God. And if Agrippa offended the crowd, he could easily create a political mess, if not an outright revolt.

It was a no-win situation for the king. The prisoner had backed him into a corner with no way out. The best thing for Agrippa to do at that point was to laugh off the question altogether—so that is exactly what he did.

Agrippa looked straight at Paul and replied, "You almost persuade me to become a Christian."

Paul held up his chained arms and instantly replied, "That's what I am praying for...." With that, the king rose, along with Bernice, Festus, and those sitting with them. They briefly conferred in another room and agreed that Paul hadn't committed anything resembling a capital crime, or even anything deserving imprisonment.

"This man might have been set free, if he had not appealed to Caesar," said a confused King Agrippa.

But Paul knew that God wanted him in Rome, and he looked forward to the opportunity. No amount of hardship, imprisonment, torture, or personal danger would keep him from his final appointment. The wheels had been set into motion.

Paul, a lowly prisoner bound in chains and completely at the mercy of Rome, prepared to board a ship that would sail out on a journey toward the epicenter of the "civilized world." As he stood on the deck of a small Adramyttium ship and watched the harbor of Caesarea—with its gleaming breakwater and impressive, colossal statues, disappear into the watery horizon—Paul must have smiled to himself at God's amazing sovereignty. Here He was, using all the resources of Rome to move the message of Jesus the Messiah from Judea to the entire world. ⚓

Chapter Fourteen

A THIRD ANCHOR

COLORADO SPRINGS, COLORADO—FEBRUARY 2002

*I*t had been little over a month since my return from Afghanistan when I got an excited call from my friend Ray in Malta. He was talking so fast, and with his thick Maltese accent, I almost couldn't understand what he was trying to say. But I did hear the words "third anchor."

"Third anchor?" I interrupted.

"Yes, Bob," he said, "There is a third anchor. I couldn't stop thinking about Tony and the other two anchors I told you about, so I did a little checking on my own. I asked the old group of divers, and several people remembered that an old diving buddy named Charles Grech had brought up an anchor from the Munxar. He brought it up with Tony shortly after we found the first two."

I hesitated a moment before asking, "Do you know where this Charles is?"

"Yes, yes," Ray said eagerly. "He owns a nice restaurant in St. Julian's. I went to see him, and he told me how he and Tony found an anchor while hunting lobster by The Bank on the Munxar. He said he found a lead anchor stock a little over five feet long, right in front of the big cave."

As Ray's excited stream of words began to slow, he added, "Bob, I would think that the only time you have three anchors together on the seafloor apart from a shipwreck is if somebody cut them away from a ship."

Typically, he explained, when an anchor is found on the sea bottom all by itself, it's the result of being snagged on a rock, like snagging a fishing line. When the anchor won't come free, it's cut.

"But *three* anchors, Bob, getting snagged at the same time, in the same place—this is hard to believe."

Ray had caught the excitement of the search for the anchors, and I could tell that he had been thinking about the proximity of the three anchors and what that meant. His logic seemed valid. And he noted something else: Solid lead anchors were extremely expensive in Roman times, just as they are now. There existed virtually no scenario in which someone, much less an experienced sea captain, would have just dropped three critically important, and *costly,* anchors and left them in the sea unless they had a mighty compelling reason. We had already explored what those reasons might be: (1) All three went down with a ship during a shipwreck—even though most shipwrecks are found on reefs or in shallower water, not in ninety feet of water as these three were reportedly found; or (2) these anchors were dropped from a ship on purpose.

On the long odds they had been dropped on purpose, it would be an unlikely coincidence, given what we already knew, for them to be found several centuries later—along the shoreline geography the Bible describes; in front of a bay with the same distinct features that the Bible lists; in the same depth of water that the Bible specifies; and of apparently the same vintage we would expect to find on a first-century Alexandrian ship like the Bible portrays. They also came to rest where "two seas meet," just as the Bible states.

Still, I had begun to ask myself what seemed to be a question crucial to determining whether these anchors had been intentionally cut loose or had gone down with a ship. If the anchors went down with a ship, for instance, then where were the *remains* of the ship? Had there been, or were there, legitimate remnants of a wreck, or a typical debris field one might expect of such an occurrence, somewhere beneath the sand near where the anchors once lay?

Entertaining the possibility that Ray, or one of the other Maltese divers, might turn up additional anchors, I had begun reading Lionel Casson's excellent book *Ships and Seafaring in Ancient Times.* In it he writes, "When an ancient vessel came to grief and landed on the seafloor, the movement of water and sand and the action of marine borers gradually destroyed the exposed parts of the hull and other elements made of organic matter...this is why no hulls of freighters carrying grain are ever found: grain was transported in bulk or in sacks, and if a ship loaded with it went to the bottom, the cargo soon vanished along with the hull."[22]

Based on this, I was fairly certain that, had a ship wrecked near the Munxar Reef, nothing of its hull or rigging would have remained after almost two thousand years. Yet other wrecks around Malta had yielded plenty of small debris: items such as clay amphorae or coins. The same would be true of the Roman freighter. I hoped to someday secure permission from the Maltese government (which is required) to search the seabed for additional clues. It would be interesting to investigate not only the area around the Big Cave but also farther toward shore, at the base of the reef where the huge grain freighter would have gotten stuck and subsequently sunk.

Ray's phone call both stirred and encouraged me. The mounting evidence caused me to wonder: If Ray had located a third anchor, perhaps the fourth and final anchor could be found as well—either still concealed on the bottom of St. Thomas Bay, or perhaps in the hands of an unknown diver. In my optimism, I even went so far as to conjecture that some of the remaining lead weights from the melted first anchor might also be tracked down. And why not? Doors that had been locked shut for two millennia now seemed to be creaking open.

As I ended my phone conversation with Ray, I asked if he might ask Charles to send me a photo of the third anchor. Ray agreed to ask, though it seemed like a long shot. I literally could not believe my eyes when, a couple of days later, photos of a Roman anchor appeared on my computer screen in an e-mail from Charles. From what we had learned about ancient anchors, Charles's anchor definitely appeared to be a first-century Roman anchor stock. Suddenly Ray and his old diving club had warmed to my theory and were cheerfully serving as amateur sleuths helping me piece together a two-thousand-year-old puzzle.

Within a few days of receiving the e-mail and photos, I called Charles and asked him if he would allow a film crew to videotape his anchor. He said he would and commented, "I never would have thought that an old anchor would be of such interest to anybody."

He hadn't yet been made privy to the source of my keen interest in his "old anchor," so I explained to Charles my theory step-by-step, starting with Paul's voyage from Caesarea, to Sidon, to Myra, to Crete, toward the shore of Africa, then finally to a point intersecting Malta in the south, in St. Thomas Bay.

I waited for a response, but all I could hear was Charles's soft breathing over the phone. And then, quite pensively, he remarked, "I do not know if I believe all that is said in the Bible, all the legends and stories. But if this is proven to be from Paul's shipwreck, it will be history." He paused. "I will need to rethink some things about this book, the Bible."

I proposed that on my next trip to Malta, I could bring experts who could examine the anchor to certify its dating and authenticity. He thought about it for a few moments, and then finally echoed concerns similar to those I had heard repeatedly from Malta's early diving fraternity. He openly feared being hit with a heavy fine, or even prison, if his anchor indeed turned out to be an ancient historical artifact. As a diver, he well knew the laws governing the discovery and full disclosure of ancient objects collected from the seafloor.

I confessed that I had no easy answer for him about legal issues and conceded that he certainly might incur difficulties from the government of Malta. I had crossed this bridge with Tony's wife, Margaret, and I knew the problem had to be solved. If these people, because of my inquiry, found themselves trapped in a publicity storm for possibly possessing anchors from Paul's shipwreck, then all of Malta, maybe even the world, would be asking how such priceless artifacts came to be in the possession of a group of Maltese spear fishermen.

MALTA, MAY 23, 2002

It took me more than a month, but I finally cleared my schedule and pulled together a research and film team. I returned to Malta with Jim

Fitzgerald and his son Jay; friends Edgar and Yvonne Miles and their son Jeremy; Jerry and Gail Nordskog; videographers Bryan Boorujy and David Stotts; and my good friend Darrell Scott (Darrell's daughter Rachel was the first student killed at the Columbine High School tragedy in Littleton, Colorado). The night after our arrival, we were seated together in a seaside restaurant in an exclusive section of Malta's St. Julian district. Our host was the restaurant's proprietor, Charles Grech—owner of the third anchor.

Charles greeted us at the door with a huge smile and an ample girth rounded from years of sampling from his well-appointed kitchen. After customary introductions, the team sat down and menus were passed around. Charles said, "Let me, if I may, suggest your meal selections."

We enjoyed a wonderful dinner, and as the group finished their meals, Charles and I made our way to a quiet table on the terrace, overlooking the bay. Without any prompting, Charles started right in.

"Tony and I found our anchor on February 10, 1972. It was the Feast of St. Paul, the day we celebrate Paul's shipwreck on Malta. I remember that day too because it was my thirty-third birthday. I started diving when I was a young man." He laughed and patted his belly. "The fish were plentiful, tourists were hungry, and business was good. One day after I had been diving for fish, a man named Tony saw me tossing my fins and mask and other diving gear in my car. Divers were few on the island in those days, so when Tony saw me putting my gear in the car, he had to meet me."

Charles recalled that Tony was with his dive buddy Joe Navarro and that the three of them became fast friends and began diving together. Over time they pitched in to buy a few Aqua-Lungs and a German rubber dinghy with an eighteen-horsepower engine and started up a little company called CTJ—for Charles, Tony, and Joe.

"We spearfished together, sold the fish to the pubs and restaurants, and started some other small commercial ventures." He pointed to the bay. "Scraping the bottoms of boats, things like that. You know, anything to make money while diving."

All the divers I'd met on this island enjoyed reminiscing about the carefree old days of youth, but most of all they liked spinning tales of all the days they spent spearfishing with Tony. A young waiter stopped by our table. "Sorry to interrupt, Mr. Grech. Would you like anything more?"

Charles casually waved his hand and asked, "Anything for you, Bob?"

"No thank you, Charles," I said, eager to hear the rest of his story.

Charles ordered a cappuccino, then looked back at me in a contemplative manner. "This is my last night at the restaurant," he said. "I've sold the old place." He turned and looked at the moored fishing boats silhouetted in the moonlight in the dark harbor and sighed, "I'm now going to just fish. I like so much to fish."

It was clear that he was feeling wistful and nostalgic, but I couldn't help myself. I steered the conversation back to the anchor. "Tell me about the day you found the anchor with Tony," I said, overly impatient to hear his story.

"Well, Bob, there had been a big storm. Afterward Tony asked me to go catch lobster with him on the Munxar. It was hard going in Malta in those days, so we did anything to make a few extra pounds. Lobsters would get the best money, and the caves on Munxar had plenty.

"Well, we were diving out on the Munxar and pulling ourselves across the rock and groping in the holes for lobster." He demonstrated by

169

thrusting his hands outward and back. "Then, there it was—this big anchor, slightly exposed through the sand. The storm probably agitated the ocean bottom, and the currents had shifted the sand to reveal a straight edge of lead. We brushed away the sand and saw just how big it was—over five feet long.

"Once we were on the surface," he continued, "Tony said that he had found other anchors at this very spot. He said we needed to go get some empty metal drums to bring the anchor up."

Charles told Tony that he had a powerful wench that could lift the anchor from the seafloor to his boat. Charles said they eventually took the barnacle-encrusted slab of lead to his own house, where the anchor began to reek in the afternoon heat. He moved it outside, and that is where it has remained to this day.

Then I heard something that was like receiving an electric shock. "There was another anchor found on the outer Munxar," Charles said, looking right at me with a locked-on stare. "The anchor," he continued, "was a big Roman achor just like mine. It was found by a man named Mario."

"A fourth anchor?!" I stammered. Excitement swirled with mental confusion. Could this really be true?

I had come a long way from being on my own shipwreck in Ethiopia to now possibly learning about a fourth and final anchor. Leaning forward with transparent eagerness, I said simply, "Charles, tell me about Mario."

Charles looked at me and saw a face that shared every bit of his own building excitement. "The day I heard about your theory, about anchors from St. Paul on the Munxar, I couldn't sleep," he said. "My mind would not rest. And then I remembered the time I found a small anchor, one that was less than two feet long, in shallow water. I brought it up, and while I was putting it into the trunk of my car, a fellow diver named Mario saw it. He laughed at how small my anchor was and asked me where I found it. I told him, and he said that he had found a large Roman stock on the Munxar, but it was much bigger than mine, over five feet long."

Charles shrugged his shoulders and laughed. "Why I remember such a short conversation from so many years ago, I don't know."

Sipping the last foam from his cappuccino, he stood up and placed his hand on my shoulder. "I don't know where this fourth anchor could be. I heard that Mario died several years ago. But I think I know of the village where he once lived. So if you want, tomorrow we can go out there and see if we can find out anything about him. If we cannot find Mario's anchor, we will still be able to see mine at my house."

Standing to shake Charles's hand, I said, "Thank you, Charles."

He was in high spirits and apparently confident. "We *will* find this fourth anchor," he said, smiling exuberantly. Then, exiting the terrace, he nudged me and pointed toward the dazzling moonlit bay. "And then we will do a little fishing!" ⚓

Chapter Fifteen

THE FOURTH ANCHOR

*E*arly the following morning, a soft rain fell from low misty clouds as we waited for Charles in the hotel lobby. Grumbling tourists had congregated around the windows, complaining about the gray soaking rain.

I paid no mind to the weather. I was anxious to get started looking for the mysterious Mario the diver of Charles's distant recollection. Shortly, Charles drove up in a white SUV, skidding to a stop on the wet driveway in front of the lobby entrance. I hopped into the car and we sped off. He seemed just as energized about our search this morning as he had been the night before.

"I did a bit of calling last night after you left," he said, wheeling the SUV out of the hotel parking lot. "I talked to an old friend who confirmed that Mario once lived in a village in the south part of Malta."

"Great, let's go!" I said, and for the next thirty minutes we swerved down a maze of narrow twisting roads, passing scooters and small cars, honking and splashing water in a tangled ballet of frenetic traffic.

We drove into a typical Maltese town with a large, Baroque-style domed church in the town's center. As we stopped and got out of the car, church bells chimed a progression of throaty *bongs,* filling the town square and beyond with a resonant, melodic hum.

I had noticed that every village in Malta revolves, in some degree or another, around churches like this one, their splendid domes dwarfing the cluster of surrounding villas and homes; their interiors adorned with gilded ceilings, ornate altars, and magnificent frescoes. Demographically speaking, about 87 percent of the people living in Malta attend church regularly, a higher percentage than in any other country in Europe. In the summer months, each church and village maintains a sort of rivalry with the other parishes, competing to see who can produce the most ornate festivals, parades, and fireworks displays.

"Where do we begin the search?" I asked Charles as he parked the car and we stepped out onto the street. We stood surrounded by a dense cluster of homes, roads, and shops.

Charles explained, "Families live in these villages five, six generations, or more. People do not move around here like they do in America. Still, this may not be so easy because there are numerous Marios living in this area."

Even so, chances were slim that many of these local Marios had been accomplished divers from the old days.

Charles walked over to a street vendor selling his wares from a small stand next to the sidewalk, his cart bulging with melons, leeks, zucchini, squash, and onions. Thinking we might be interested in his produce, the roadside merchant held up two large squash for our inspection. Charles immediately began his inquiry about a man named Mario who was a diver thirty years ago. After a short conversation in Maltese punctuated by several quick exchanges of nodding and talking, the merchant motioned, using a squash as a pointer, toward a door directly behind us. We turned to see the entrance to an older quaint Mediterranean villa, constructed in traditional Maltese style: a pleasing, two-story facade abutting the narrow sidewalk running in front of a long row of buildings.

"Who lives here?" I asked Charles as we stepped up to the door.

Charles smiled broadly. "The man explained that this is where 'Mario the diver' lived—and that his widow still lives here today."

As I tried to fathom this seemingly unbelievable merging of chance and coincidence, Charles rang the doorbell. From the balcony above us, wooden shutters opened and a woman leaned over the railing. She shouted something to Charles in Maltese, and after a short, animated conversation, the woman disappeared and soon reappeared, opening the heavy front door. There, from a thin gap in the doorway, she continued her lively dialogue with Charles in English (I assumed Charles had told her I was an American).

"Hello," she said. "Can I help you?"

Charles smiled politely and replied, "I was one of Mario's good friends many years ago. You and I were once at a wedding together."

"Oh yes, yes," she said with a look of doubtful recognition. I took her to be Mario's wife, or a close relative—a sister perhaps. As the conversation progressed, she nudged the door open wider.

"I'm sorry for the way I must look," she said, patting her hair with an air of embarrassment. "I was not expecting visitors today."

Charles said, "We have something very important to ask you." Justifiably confused by our sudden appearance at her doorstep, she seemed a bit puzzled but nonetheless swayed by the urgency in Charles's

175

voice. Opening the door the rest of the way, she waved us into her entry hall and pointed to a side parlor.

"Please come in and be seated. I will be with you in a moment."

She disappeared up the stairs, leaving us in a room decorated with antique pots, old nautical maps, and ancient treasures. Within five minutes she reappeared, smoothing her dress and patting her freshly brushed hair. Seating herself in an antique wooden chair directly in front of us, she took a deep breath and said, "I can listen to you now. Please go on."

"I was sorry to hear about Mario," Charles said.

So she was Mario's wife.

"He died twenty years ago," the woman responded with a pained smile. She tilted her head, reminded of the memory, and sadly raised her eyebrows.

Glancing my way, Charles explained to her, "This is Bob Cornuke, from America. He is here in Malta researching an ancient shipwreck—a very important old shipwreck."

The woman (she later asked that she and her husband remain anonymous, so I have changed his name) turned to me and asked, "Did Mario have something to do with the shipwreck you are speaking about?"

I measured my words, realizing I stood in the presence of perhaps the only person alive who could direct us to the fourth and final anchor. "He may have," I replied slowly. "Do you know if Mario ever spoke of bringing up a large Roman-style anchor from the seafloor?"

"Yes," she answered, "I know that Mario brought up such an anchor. I think it was in the late sixties, but I can't be sure about that."

I swallowed. "Do you know what he did with this anchor?"

"Yes."

Expecting her to elaborate, I hesitated a moment and then asked, "Does this anchor exist *today* in Malta?"

"Yes," she replied again, without emotion.

"Do you know where it is?"

"Yes."

I took a deep breath. Did I dare ask her the next logical question, knowing her answer held enormous implications for our entire mission? I paused a moment and decided to forge ahead. "Can you show us that anchor?"

Standing up from her chair, Mario's widow invited us through a doorway into the bright sunshine. We rose to follow her outside, where sporadic raindrops fell from a few remaining scraps of cloud, yielding patches of brilliant blue sky. She motioned to a short wall in the courtyard, and there, resting in front of her garden, lay a huge Roman anchor stock.

She didn't seem to grasp the magnitude of what she possessed, but said simply, "It is too big to keep in the house." For several moments the three of us stood staring at the precious lead treasure. Charles wore a glazed look of stunned amazement, muttering below his breath, "It looks just like my anchor...the same size, the same color." He jerked around to look me in the eye. "This could be *my* anchor, Bob. It is my anchor's...*twin.*"

The stock was a long, rectangular solid lead casting rendered in the identical Roman/Alexandrian motif as the others. It had the telltale square center hole, which once held a huge wooden shaft; the two arms together spanned over five feet, radiating out from the hollow square center. Neither arm was perfectly straight; each had a slight bow in the lead.

Kneeling down, I ran my hand over its wet, barnacle encrusted side. It was cool to the touch. Then I steadied myself and strained against its bulk to test its weight, but I couldn't even budge it. Before me sat a massive monolith, stone cold and immovable, whose size, weight, and potential biblical significance struck me with awe.

I stood up and asked, "Do you know where Mario found this anchor?"

"I remember Mario saying that he found the anchor on the Munxar," she said, "or maybe on the island of Camino. Mario was one of the first divers in Malta, and he found many objects in the sea. But as far as this anchor, I am not sure where my husband found it. I only remember him saying something about the Munxar or Camino." She closed her eyes for a moment, dredging her memory, but looked up and said, "I'm sorry that I can't be more specific for you."

I could see that she badly wanted to tell me exactly where her husband had found this anchor, but too much time had passed and nothing was left of the distant conversation she had had with him about his find.

Still, I needed to be certain about this anchor. As incredible as the anchor was, its origin remained a mystery. All I knew for sure was the woman's vague "it may have come from here or there." *Had it come from the Munxar as had the other three?* The chances seemed fairly bright: If two of the three other anchors had survived intact almost two thousand years, then the fourth anchor could have lasted until now as well.

Or had this anchor been lost to the seafloor during some other ship's misfortune on the unforgiving rocks around Malta? Maybe it had snagged on the sea bottom and had been cut loose by another huge ship somewhere on the island of Camino, far removed from the Munxar Reef. Or, just maybe, it was indeed the fourth anchor we were looking for.

Standing in the garden, I stared silently at the anchor at my feet, wishing it could speak. I didn't know, in that moment, where I might find the answers to the questions that raced through my brain. But experience had taught me that somewhere, somehow, *someone* knew where Mario had found this anchor. ⚓

Chapter Sixteen

THE WINDS OF FATE

*T*he excitement of the past two days—meeting Charles, tracking down Mario the diver's widow, and locating the possible fourth anchor—had distracted me from the very thing I had come to Malta to do. I still hadn't seen the anchor Charles said he had raised from the Munxar Reef in 1972. As anxious as I was to see it, I didn't want to do so without the benefit of Professor Anthony Bonanno's expert opinion. On a prior trip, Malta Professor Bonanno (head of the Department of Archeology at the University of Malta) had graciously viewed video clips of Tony Micallef-Borg's anchor (chapter 10). If anyone could verify the authenticity and dating of Roman anchors, it would be Professor Bonanno.

The morning after visiting with the widow of Mario the diver and seeing what we hoped might be anchor four, I met up with Professor Bonanno and the rest of the research team and drove to Charles's home to see his alleged Roman anchor. (Perhaps prematurely, we had already taken to calling it "the third anchor.")

We met Charles at his house and made introductions all around, then waited as he excused himself to retrieve the anchor. After a few minutes he reappeared, straining to push a wheeled dolly on which sat a huge lead anchor stock—a mirror image of the stock we had seen the day before in the garden of Mario's widow. We rushed over to help him move the anchor out where we could see it in the sunlight.

With all of us struggling to maneuver the dolly outside, I asked Charles, "How in the world did you get this thing onto the dolly?"

He laughed. "It took *five* of us—four young men plus myself—to even lift it."

As Professor Bonanno began to examine the anchor, our entire team wrestled it off the dolly so he could get a better look. Even with several full-grown men pushing and heaving, it barely moved. *How in the world, I thought, could anyone retrieve this metal monster out of the sea?*

Finally Professor Bonanno knelt down and placed his hand on it.

"Where was *this* anchor found?" he asked, looking around at the group.

Charles stepped forward and said, "A man named Tony and I found this anchor thirty years ago. It was sitting on the seafloor, where I have now heard that two other anchors, and possibly a fourth, were also found."

Turning his gaze back to the anchor, Professor Bonanno inquired, "Four anchors at the *same location?*"

"Yes," said Charles. "They were brought up from the Munxar Reef off St. Thomas Bay."

Bending down, Professor Bonanno took the next several minutes to examine the anchor up close, from every conceivable angle. Finally he stood up to address us as a group, his tone and demeanor deadpan and professorial, as though he was teaching in his classroom at the University.

"What I am looking at is clearly a solid lead anchor stock, a stock of a Roman anchor," he explained. "A Roman anchor consisted mostly of a wooden structure, with two lead parts. The most important part was the lead upper bracket, which is called the 'anchor stock.' This object here is a typical Roman anchor stock. The wooden stem would have come out of this square hole in the center. It bends on one side in one direction and on the opposite side in a different direction in order to allow the anchor to grip the seabed. The lead anchor stock is what you find in the sea because the wooden parts usually rot away."

He turned and glanced again at the ancient object and then said matter-of-factly, "This type of anchor would have been quite common during the period from the first century B.C. to the first century A.D. If one finds marks on an anchor stock, one can be even more specific. Sometimes they will have the name of the owner of the ship, allowing one to identify the owner and perhaps trace to specific dates. I have tried to look for special marks that might permit us to date this stock more exactly, but I don't see any in this state of preservation. Perhaps when one removes the encrustation we may find identifying marks."

I asked the professor whether or not he felt that this anchor stock was consistent with the type of anchor that could be aboard an Alexandrian grain freighter such as the one that carried the apostle Paul to Malta.

I felt my jaw tighten, and the professor continued. "It could have belonged to a cargo ship, possibly a grain cargo ship, and possibly one from Alexandria. Such ships used to ply the Mediterranean from Alexandria to Rome." He rubbed his eyes as though searching his memory. "Egypt was one of the granaries of Rome, and we know from sources that occasionally such ships did stop at Malta. We know of two cases where Alexandrian ships came to Malta; both are described in the Bible. One of the ships, of course, was the ship that wrecked with St. Paul onboard.

Paul stayed on the island of Malta for three months; then another Alexandrian ship took him on to Rome."

As we absorbed his analysis, Professor Bonanno slapped his hands together, shaking loose some residue from the anchor's encrusted surface. Then he turned to me and said without emotion or inflection, "This anchor stock would fit very well within the era of St. Paul."

I took my small video camera out of my bag, opened the viewing screen, and showed Professor Bonanno video clips of the other anchor stocks (Ray and Tony's anchor, and Mario's). After watching video of both anchors, Professor Bonanno said, "From what I can tell from these videos —again without the benefit of physical examination—these other two anchors also appear to be typical Roman anchor stocks, appropriate to the era of St. Paul's shipwreck in Malta."

THE DRIFT

That night, I was notified that a high-level military official had granted us a rare opportunity. Amazingly, we had been given permission to have access to, and use of, a very expensive and sophisticated computer program that was being used by the Rescue Coordination Center of the Armed Forces of Malta.

This was both exciting and providential because this multimillion-dollar computer program had the high-tech ability to determine the drift of Paul's ship across the Mediterranean. Twenty-first-century technology was about to bridge an ancient gulf of uncertainty. The computer would objectively speak to us across the millennia and trace the, until now, uncertain path of the biblical event of Paul's journey from Crete to Malta. We would soon learn with reasonable certainty the uncharted course Paul and his fellow shipmates took in that terror-filled tempest over nineteen hundred years ago.

The next day we met with Major Manuel Mallia at the Headquarters of the Armed Forces of Wartime. Major Mallia was in charge of Air and Maritime Operations. He explained that we were at the Operations Center of the Armed Forces of Malta, which serves, among other things, as the Search and Rescue Coordination Center for Malta. The scope of their responsibility was revealed by his statement, "Our search and rescue region encompasses approximately a quarter of a million square kilometers, servicing a vast portion of the entire Mediterranean Sea."

I surveyed the operations center. Several men stood intently monitoring consoles, navigational charts, plasma-screen TVs, and radar screens, which lined the walls. Had this high-tech rescue center existed nearly two thousand years ago, these men would have received a distress call from the Roman freighter upon which Paul sailed. In response, they would have dispatched helicopters and sea rescue vessels, all the while listening to the frantic cries of the captain ordering equipment overboard and cables run beneath the ship to keep the swells from pounding the craft to pieces.

I had read of other disastrous shipwrecks in that era, when mishaps at sea were an all too common occurrence. In one account, the ancient historian Synesius described the following terror:

> The men groaned, the women shrieked, everybody called upon God, cried aloud, remembered their dear ones.... I noticed that the soldiers had all drawn their swords. I asked why and learned that they preferred to

belch up their souls to the open air, on deck, rather than gurgle them up to the sea.... Then someone called out that all who had any gold should hang it around their neck. Those who had did so, both gold and anything else of the value of gold. The women not only put on their jewelry but handed out pieces of string to any who needed them. This is a time-honoured practice, and the reason for it is this: you must provide the corpse of someone lost at sea with the money to pay for a funeral so that whoever recovers it, profiting by it, won't mind giving it a little attention....[23]

Even Josephus, the renowned historian of the first century A.D., endured a similar ordeal at sea. He wrote:

Accordingly I came to Rome, though it were through a great number of hazards, by sea; for, as our ship sank in the Adriatic [Mediterranean] Sea, we that were in it, being about six hundred in number, swam for our lives all the night; when, upon the first appearance of the day, and upon our sight of a ship of Cyrene, I and some others, eighty in all, by God's providence, survived....[24]

Standing in the Search and Rescue Center, I had to wonder how they would have handled such situations in ancient times: like the swamping of Josephus's ship, or of Paul's running aground on their island. As I admired the wealth of sophisticated equipment, Major Mallia informed me that he could use the Center's Search and Rescue computer system to model the precise circumstances leading up to Paul's shipwreck.

"This morning we are using our software to calculate drift against time of a hypothetical search object—in this case, the object will be the Alexandrian freighter that carried St. Paul. We define the known parameters, then input the appropriate data, such as the approximate size of the vessel, the days at sea, and the weather conditions as defined in the Bible. The computer will then calculate the probable drift of our search object."

He had my full attention. "Can you explain to me how it works?" I asked.

"Let's say you drop a corked bottle with a message in it off the coast of Crete. The computer can process the weather patterns during that time period, the currents of the ocean, the weight and drag coefficient of the bottle, and then calculate where that object would be in a day, two days, three days, and so on, depending on the given data.

"It is no different with a ship," he added with a shrug. "If we take a ship that was in a gregale and start it at a given point, we can calculate where it would go. The computer possesses millions of calculations on existing sea currents in the Mediterranean and has proven quite accurate in determining weather patterns, especially those weather patterns from annual storm systems."

The major explained that northeasters are most common in the Mediterranean and that the rescue center has amassed massive volumes of data pertaining to weather characteristics during these types of storm occurrences. The major walked us over to a console containing a large computer screen.

"What we will do," he explained, "is ask the computer to find a large wooden vessel meeting the general parameters of a grain freighter from the time of Paul. We can even input the type of hull—its *wood type*—and then take into account the veering characteristics of a northeaster, adding to it the leeway of time and the history of currents during the fall season when this incident would have occurred."

Staring into the screen, the major said softly, "We will start the computer program after I input all the pertinent data."

With my Bible open, I explained where the ship of Paul had been traveling at the time the storm blew it off course.

"The ship was going from a port called Fair Havens," I began, "traveling along the southern coast of Crete, going in a westerly direction. The Bible says that a 'favorable south wind' occurred, suggesting that the ship was probably going around the Cape Matala when it was suddenly slammed hard by a northeaster, today referred to as a gregale." I told him that the last known coordinate of Paul's ship came off of the southern coast of the small island of Clauda, where in a desperate attempt to save the ship, the sailors pulled the skiff onboard and undergirded the ship with cables.

As we began to input the data, an alarm suddenly sounded over the loudspeakers, indicating that one of the center's many daily rescues was commencing. The major turned to me casually and said, "We have an incident. We can no longer continue the computer program. I'm sorry, but if you could return tomorrow, we will finish then."

As we hastily gathered our gear to leave, the big flat-screen TV mounted in the search operations center showed a live black-and-white video feed of helicopters circling a stricken vessel in the middle of the Mediterranean. The dilapidated vessel was being tossed about in huge swells and fierce wind some two hundred miles off the coast of Malta.

Before we left the Search and Rescue Center, the major stopped me and said, "You know, our tradition on Malta says that Paul's ship ended up in St. Paul's Bay." Then he smiled. "Tomorrow the computer will answer the question of the direction in which Paul drifted in the storm the Bible describes."

THE DEFINING MOMENT

The next day we returned to the center. It was a beautiful day, the wind calm and the sea relatively smooth and flat. Upon entering Major Mallia's office, we were greeted with a warm reassurance: "The weather looks okay until later in the afternoon, when the wind picks up and the seas get rough."

We returned to the sophisticated array of equipment, which Major Mallia proudly announced had been donated by the United States Coast Guard following an extensive bilateral training course. The major explained that the new Operations Center in which we were sitting was only three weeks old. The room, in fact, smelled of new paint, rubber, and plastic.

It felt to me like a defining moment. Much was at stake for me personally. The equation was simple: If the computer determined a northerly drift, it would *eliminate* my primary search site. If, however, it calculated a southerly drift, the helplessly drifting ship would have impacted the southeast coast of Malta, aligning perfectly with the Munxar Reef theory. Depending on the outcome, this exercise could also put in grave question the possibility that Paul's ship ever could have landed anywhere on the northern coast of Malta—more specifically, the traditional site of St. Paul's Bay.

The major began to input the data directly out of the Bible and then simulated a northeasterly storm system as described in the Book of Acts.

"Now we will see," he said, turning to me. "Each quadrant in our computation comprises a forty-eight-hour period of drift. The massive amount of data takes some time to compute. It is, however, as accurate as we can possibly get."

Our team crowded around the major's chair to watch. A version of history never before seen now unfolded before us. As the first forty-eight hours of drift appeared on the screen, it showed Paul's ship traveling in a westerly direction from the lee of the tiny island of Clauda. At that point, it looked like it would be a coin toss whether it would then go north or south. However, as the next forty-eight hours began to plot on the screen, it showed Paul's ship veering sharply to the south in a steady, wind-driven drift. The next several quadrants of the program, in fact, showed the ship missing the northern coast of Africa by as little as seventy-eight miles. No wonder the sailors aboard Paul's ship were so frightened! To strike and shipwreck on that coastline would have been certain disaster. Without water available to them for hundreds of miles, they would have been over-taken by thirst and succumbed to a miserable death.

To explain why the ship didn't strike the African coastline, some Bible translations describe a sort of drag mechanism being deployed at or near this junction, in the ship's out-of-control movement. More than likely, a sheet of sail in the shape of a windsock was used to slow the ship's rate of progress and artificially steer it back out to sea. The text in its original Greek literally says that the sailors "let down [from above] the vessel, and in this way were driven." Interestingly, this same type of emergency sea anchor/parachute is still used by sailors today in catastrophic storms.

The computer labored on according to the raw data, its soft-glowing screen flickering digital updates of the route taken by Paul's ship as it was driven by the storm. Major Mallia kept looking back at me as the process unfolded and muttering, "This is surprising to me. Very… *surprising.*" Staring into the screen, he had become totally focused on the events playing out before him. Finally, whispering to himself, he said, "This computer is quite accurate. The conditions we have inputted are as close as we can assess the conditions at the time of Paul." Then he took a slow, deep breath and said, "I never could have imagined that the vessel's drift would come…from the *south* as you had surmised."

Over the next half hour, the computer continued to generate forty-eight-hour quadrants, ultimately showing the ship intersecting Malta. Turning toward the major, I asked, "Precisely where would Paul's ship have been at the end of fourteen days?"

He looked back at the screen and then down at his data files. "The computer shows the object striking Malta sometime in the late evening or the early morning hours of the fourteenth day."

Acts 27:27 tells us, "On the *fourteenth* night we were still being driven across the Adriatic Sea, when about midnight the sailors sensed they were approaching land."

With my heart rate increasing, I then asked, "Where does the drift show the object hitting Malta?"

Very slowly, very deliberately, the major said, "This dotted line is within the area where we would expect the drift object to be. *Anywhere* on that line." Tracing a finger across the screen, he said, "…that line hits Malta on the *south,* where we also find the Munxar Reef."

Neither of us, or any member of our team, could find words to express the significance of the computer's findings. As we slowly allowed the major's words to settle in our minds, he softly and deliberately confirmed our theory.

"The spine of the Munxar Reef is shallow, going perpendicular to the land, more than a mile off shore. In a storm like the one described in the Bible, it would be treacherous. Knowing the way heavy, steel-plated ships can be wrecked on it, I hate to imagine what would happen to a wooden ship colliding with the jagged stony jaws of the Munxar Reef. There's no way any ancient ship could have survived." Then, as if thinking aloud, he recalled, "Behind the Munxar Reef is a sandy beach, and the currents in a storm system as described in the Bible would eventually wash anything wrecked on the reef onto that beach."

Finally, unable to ignore the pregnant silence, the major turned, looked me in the eye, and said simply, *"It is surprising even to me!"*

Everyone in the Search and Rescue Area stood in stunned silence, staring at the computer screen. After the initial excitement of watching the arc of the ship cross the computer screen, the final verdict struck me as neither somber nor exciting.

As in other investigations I had undertaken around the world, the converging pieces of the puzzle amid the longest odds brought only a feeling of thankful relief. I knew that, while even such a sophisticated software program can be fallible, what stood before us is the best available technology to realistically model what happened to Paul's ship.

The computer program confirmed that the ship must have had come from the south and that its drift had completely eliminated St. Paul's Bay and other bays closely associated with it as the possible landing site. That left only two realistic candidates as the ship's possible landfall: St. Thomas Bay or Marsaxlokk Bay. Of these two, even Major Mallia agreed that only St. Thomas Bay possessed all the physical, nautical, and geographical conditions that aligned perfectly with the Bible's description.

ANOTHER SHIP MAYBE?

Even though the evidence was mounting that the anchors from the Munxar were from the ship of Paul, I had to consider the fact that another ship totally unrelated to Paul's might have sunk at the exact same spot. But given maritime logic, that notion seemed beyond the scope of probability.

The captain of Paul's ship had arrived off the coast of Malta, drifting out of control in the dead of night. The crew heard waves crashing in the darkness somewhere off the bow. The captain then quickly ordered the sailors to determine the depth of the sea by dropping a lead weight attached to a rope into the water. When he found out that the seafloor was receding in depth, he ordered four huge lead anchors cast in the sea from the stern. He did not have the benefit of choosing the best place to anchor on the coastline. In fact, when morning arrived, he learned that he had anchored at an extremely perilous spot. Would a seasoned sea captain choose to anchor directly in front of a reef being pounded by surf? He wouldn't have.

Could another ship with anchors from the era of Paul sink where the anchors were found on the Munxar? Most likely not. Close to shore, a ship almost always sinks from hitting rocks or a reef. The keel depth of a large wooden ship would not be able to hit the rocks ninety feet down, which is the depth that the Munxar anchors were found. Those anchors that were found thirty-five years ago by young Maltese divers on the outer Munxar were sent to the bottom by men who dropped them from a ship—not from a ship that sank.

Often in this type of investigation, gaping holes remain that need to be addressed, things that cannot, from all available evidence, be explained. But that didn't seem to be the case in this investigation. We not only had three, possibly four, of the anchors dated to the time of Paul; we also had computerized verification of the Munxar Reef's statistical probability as the shipwreck site.

Other critical details lined up as well: The anchors had been found in the approximate depth of water of which the Bible speaks; they struck bottom where "two seas meet"; and finally, they came to rest at a spot between the reef and the shore—a reef that would have been at a depth to allow Paul's ship to run aground and get the bow stuck and the stern submerged. Then, of course, there was a bay with a beach. No other possible place on Malta fit all of these criteria.

The exciting theory was now fusing with the reality of mounting coincidence. Several months prior, I had corresponded with Dr. Chuck Missler and posed the very question of the mathematical probabilities of another ship in history encountering all the unique circumstances of the Munxar Reef scenario intersecting with the biblical narrative.

Chuck Missler, a Ph.D., has had a thirty-year career developing high technology enterprises and has also served as a senior analyst for think tanks in the intelligence community. He would offer a unique perspective on the mathematical calculation of probability on the Munxar Reef findings as it relates to Luke's description from the Bible. Dr. Missler computed all the historical criteria of Paul's shipwreck, including drift direction, geological conditions, and the distinctive descriptions such as where "two seas meet," sea depth, the typology of the anchors, etc. His opinion was as follows:

Any attempt to estimate the a priori mathematical composite probabilities of encountering all the unique concatenation of the specific details you describe in relation to the Biblical text would clearly exceed the threshold of absurdity. (In mathematical physics, the threshold of absurdity, as required for the integration of asymptotic function, is defined as a probability of less than 10^{-50}. In the case of anchors, the inferred composite probability easily exceeds this, even without an application of Bayes' Theorem, etc.)

I asked Dr. Missler to put his opinion in simpler terms. His response was, "If you have four anchors, in the specific place you described, with all the specific criteria, then this is Paul's shipwreck."

The fourth anchor was now becoming all too important. Was it really a brother of the other three, or had it been found on some other reef and was therefore totally unrelated to our scenario?

It would have been easy enough to adopt a best-case scenario and call it good, but that would have thereafter left an open question. I had to keep working until I knew for sure about the mysterious fourth anchor.

WALKING IN ANCIENT ROME

On my last day in Malta on this third trip, I found myself strolling the lot that served as a set for the movie *The Gladiator*—an expensive, elaborate façade built to create a world of cinematic illusion. On the big screen, the set conjured up the sweeping splendor of imperial Rome; up close, it was little more than a hollow mask of wood, paint, and fading plaster.

Slowly making my way down a vacant Roman street lined with propped-up plywood walls, I pictured the set teeming with actors and cameramen. Now the only thing that moved was a piece of loose canvas flapping in the arid afternoon breeze. Exploring these modern-day ruins, I saw again how cruel time is to the worlds we construct for ourselves. Monuments fall, buildings crumble, and kings and emperors who once inspired fear are now so many specks of decaying dust—all the might that was once unrivaled Rome now reduced to crumbling columns and museum trinkets.

Along for the tour was an American film team headed by my good friend Jim Fitzgerald, who had come to Malta scouting locations for a video documentary about Paul's lost shipwreck. Lagging far behind the group, I found myself in an eerie moment of silent reflection, struggling to envision the Rome that Paul had encountered as a prisoner more than nineteen centuries ago.

Stranded on Malta for three months after the shipwreck, Paul sailed once more for Rome as a prisoner aboard yet another Alexandrian grain freighter, this one having wintered on Malta. Arriving finally in Rome, Paul must have gazed up at the imposing buildings as he was led through the city center. The Rome of Paul's day was of a scale and grandeur seen nowhere else in the world.

The streets would have been filled with throngs of people, noisy animals, and rattling carts—a bustling ethnic blend of freemen, slaves, citizens, emperors, aristocrats, and politicians. The citizens of Rome had an undisguised arrogance, deeming themselves civilized, merciful, and pious. Of course their enemies rarely lived long enough to offer an opposing opinion. Romans boasted of their civility, yet savored the sight of blood. Beast and man fought to the death in great public spectacles routinely staged in Rome's finest arenas. Once, history reveals, Caesar Augustus staged a gladiator show featuring ten thousand men; on another occasion, 260 lions and thirty-six crocodiles died to satisfy the bloodlust of the Roman population.[25]

Hardly intimidated by the spectacle buzzing around him, Paul knew that God had a high calling in store for him in Rome; he took courage in the fact his life lay not in Caesar's hands, but in God's alone. He may have been a prisoner in chains, but several months before, in the stillness of the Antonia Tower, Paul had heard the voice of Jesus in the Roman barracks in Jerusalem: "You have witnessed for me in Jerusalem; you must witness for Me in Rome."

Paul had no particular wish, desire, or plan to venture to Rome; he did so at his Lord's good pleasure. Ironically, his all-expense-paid trip to Rome occupied a rather obscure moment in history, yet the ember he ignited upon the spiritual deadwood of an unbelieving world still burns today.

The Bible provides us with only fifteen verses about Paul's visit to Rome. Oddly, once Paul arrived in Rome, there are no more Scriptures reporting stirring sermons or court dissertations; no more riots, no more mobs, no more beatings. Rather, Luke records that Paul was granted the privilege of a private residence and a soldier to guard him. In the course of his stay, Paul summoned the Jewish leaders to his house, and when the curious crowd arrived, they were kept there from morning until evening as Paul spoke about his Lord and Savior. At the end of that long day of listening to Paul share the Good News, some were persuaded by what they heard, while some disbelieved, arguing amongst themselves as they left.

*So when they did not agree among themselves, they
departed after Paul had said one word: "The Holy Spirit
spoke rightly through Isaiah the prophet to our fathers,
saying, 'Go to this people and say: "Hearing you will
hear, and shall not understand; and seeing you will see,
and not perceive."'"* (Acts 28:25–26)

Then, as today, some people simply would not see, hear, understand,
or perceive. I knew that, as with other biblical discoveries, even empirical
evidence from the paradigm of history would fail to convince some skeptics.
To these, the only evidence that matters is the court of public opinion,
which says, under no circumstances can the Bible, much less Jesus' own
claims or Paul's compelling testimony, ever be true.

I knew that when we presented the anchor story to the world, many
would simply discount it. I understand this. It is predictable. But like Paul
on his final mission trip, we have been granted a privilege of discovery
that we are now compelled to present at face value. From here, people
must make up their own minds. The experience of Paul and the other
apostles demonstrated that, always, some will believe and some will not.

It is in Rome that the story of Acts ends. Paul remained under
house arrest for two more years, though the rest of his life became
something of a mystery. Today we are uncertain as to what specific circumstances ensued and are left to piece together a picture from fragments
of second-, third-, and fourth-hand writings about him. A probable
scenario has Paul being released from house arrest in about 63 A.D.,
from which he more than likely visited Spain and the area of the Aegean.
From the Letter of Clement (95 A.D.), the Muratorian Canon (170 A.D.)

and the apocryphal Acts of Peter (200 A.D.),[26] we can reasonably surmise that, shortly thereafter, he was rearrested and put to death at the hand of Nero in about 67 A.D.

So it was that this shipwreck—this odyssey in chains across the Mediterranean, through a monstrous storm, and onto the rocks of southeast Malta—claimed just one chapter in a chain of life-shaping events the Lord ordered for Paul. Surviving a shipwreck and spending the winter on Malta filled but a short interval as Paul completed his ministry and faced his own death.

In my unexpected search for four lost sea anchors, I had been irreversibly swept up in the panorama of one man's complete commitment to Christ—a life so completely surrendered to his calling that he could write, at a time before his execution,

> *For I am already being poured out as a drink offering, and the time of my departure is at hand. I have fought the good fight, I have finished the race, I have kept the faith. Finally, there is laid up for me the crown of righteousness, which the Lord, the righteous Judge, will give to me on that Day, and not to me only but also to all who have loved His appearing.* (2 Timothy 4:6–8)

To some, the journey of Paul is good fodder for an inspirational sermon on Sunday morning or encouragement in times of severe trial. To skeptics, the account is one among a dusty compilation of old stories, little more than myth and legend relegated to the heap of endless literary fantasies.

To me, the account in Acts of the shipwreck of Paul became nothing less than an eyewitness account from a chronically accurate historian named Luke. And through my encounter with Paul's shipwreck and the artifacts of history—and, ultimately, with the man himself—I sensed I would never be the same.

I heard the group hollering for me in the distance. Their work at the set was done, so I made my way back to the van and we returned to the hotel. In the months ahead I would wonder about the anchor found by Mario the diver. Was this the fourth anchor, or was it brought up some other place? Was it the last piece of the puzzle that I was looking for? Or was it lost at sea by some other ancient vessel, only to be found by Mario somewhere known only to him? Would its original whereabouts be hidden from me forever? ⚓

Chapter Seventeen

GRANDFATHER
OF MALTA DIVERS

*I*t took me another six months to plan my fourth trip to Malta. The unsolved mystery of the so-called fourth anchor had, during the interim, kept me awake nights, dangling like a loose thread in the investigation. Leaving Malta the last time, I had been able to confirm eyewitness testimony linking the first three anchors to the Munxar Reef. All we knew for certain about the critical fourth anchor, however, was that it had been discovered by Mario the diver *somewhere* in the waters off Malta.

Interestingly enough, upon arriving back in Malta again, the rain was falling, just like my first trip, which seemed remarkable for an island with such a traditionally arid climate. The long hot days of summer had passed, and now a fall storm was drenching the almost deserted beaches and outdoor cafés. The tourists, it seemed, had gone home to Europe to toil in their jobs through the cold, damp winter, working to pay for next summer's warm Maltese holiday.

Meeting me at the airport was my good friend Ray Ardizzone, a familiar face from many of my prior expeditions. He was the one who led the prayer before our last-minute rescue on stormy Lake Tana two years earlier. That shipwreck in Ethiopia was the epiphany that launched me on this quest to begin with. Ray had been a faithful confidant and counselor, so it was appropriate that he accompany me on this last leg to track down the certainty of the fourth anchor being a brother of the other three.

Only weeks earlier I had received a phone call from Charles Grech (the man who found the third anchor with Tony), alerting me of rumors he'd heard from other divers on the island that a man named Wilfred Perotta knew where the fourth anchor had been found.

The first thing I did on landing in Malta was to contact the local police authorities and ask them for help in obtaining the phone number of one Wilfred Perotta. Wasting no time, I called the number and Wilfred answered the phone. I briefly explained my interest in finding information about Mario the diver and told him a bit about my theory on Paul's anchors. Wilfred replied with a simple, "Why not?" He invited me to come to his home to discuss the matter. One day later, Ray and I found ourselves shaking hands with this man who we hoped might know the secrets surrounding the fourth anchor.

At sixty-five years young, Wilfred's grip felt like a vise. Simply to look at him, one could see that he was a man of incredible physical condition, still working the piers, diving beneath ships, doing repairs and maintenance. On the island, Wilfred had long been known as the grandfather of all divers, one of the first three men ever to dive in the waters of Malta using oxygen canisters. At one time, like Tony, he was the underwater spearfishing champion of Malta. Walking through Wilfred's house was like entering an exotic museum, filled in no small part by his numerous diving trophies, which he proudly showed me. In 1960 he became the first athlete to win the sportsman of the year award on Malta, having participated in five world underwater spearfishing championships. A year before that, in 1959, he established a record, which will probably never be broken, during the world underwater spearfishing championship held in Malta. As impossible at it sounds, Wilfred speared six fish with just one shot.

His house was stuffed with artifacts that had been harvested from the sea. Thousands of unique seashells lined the walls, and diving gear from the pioneering days of scuba diving were all around. On his living room coffee table sat stacks of scrapbooks filled with fading photos and press clippings, even one showing a proud Wilfred receiving an award from Jacques Cousteau. Flipping open one of the many scrapbooks, I noticed that the pictures were invariably of Wilfred standing, speargun in hand, with several of his diving companions, mounds of fish at their feet.

Pausing at a picture of himself posing over a particularly large grouper, Wilfred laughed. "Today when someone finds a grouper that is three kilos, they claim it is a *big* fish. But we speared forty-kilo grouper many times."

On another page were pictures of Wilfred in various settings with Mario the diver. I saw a shadow of sadness sweep over his face as he remarked, "Mario was a good friend. We dove together all the time." He paused. "Mario died twenty years ago. We shared many good memories."

I didn't mean to be blunt, but I had to ask. "Did Mario ever tell you about an anchor he found on the Munxar?"

"Yes," he said, seeming not the least bit surprised by my question. "He told me that he brought it up with some other divers. I can't remember who they were. But I do remember Mario telling me that he hoisted up a massive anchor from out on the Munxar some time in the late sixties."

"Do you know exactly where he would have been on the Munxar?" I asked.

"He liked to dive twenty to thirty meters in depth—that's where the big groupers are on the Munxar," he explained. "That is probably where it was brought up, but we don't know for certain. The only thing for absolute certain is that he told me that he was out on the outer Munxar Reef when he found the large anchor."

I asked him if he had ever seen this Roman anchor. He told me that he had. "It's now at the home of Mario's widow, in the courtyard area," he said. That was the moment that I knew it: We now had four anchors from the Munxar location—four large anchors that appear to be consistent with the era of Paul's shipwreck.

Before I could ask another question, Wilfred stood up, turned on his television set, and slid in a videotape for me to watch. He had shot a spool of eight-millimeter film of those early days on Malta, when he was a young man, and had recently converted it to videotape. Even though I had at least a dozen more questions to ask about the fourth anchor, I relented to Wilfred's desire to share a chapter from his youth, sat back, and enjoyed the show. Over the next half hour, he took me on a sentimental journey of the diving lifestyle that he, Ray, Tony, and all the others had so loved and apparently still longed for.

"These are the earliest images of underwater diving in Malta we know of," he remarked, as the scratchy frames started flashing in the darkened room.

Watching the rare video, I became perplexed. "Wilfred, how in the world did you get film in 1956?" I asked, knowing they didn't have underwater cameras available to the public at that time. "And even if underwater cameras were available, how could you afford one?"

"Simple," he said. "I took an old watertight fuse box about eight inches by four inches by four inches and used it as a housing unit for one of the first underwater cameras. The fuse box had a small watertight glass plate on the front, and I placed my eight-millimeter windup camera inside."

As Wilfred narrated the flickering eight-millimeter film, he reminisced about the high-spirited, carefree days of Malta's diving pioneers. The homemade movie revealed in raw detail a brotherhood of young, athletic divers who reveled in the camaraderie and sport of their newly adopted vocation. Loaded down with primitive diving gear and rudimentary spearguns, Wilfred and his friends chased and speared trophy-sized groupers, brought them topside, and eventually strung the fish from a heavy wooden pole that sagged under the weight of the catch.

I had heard so many dramatic stories of these daring cowboy divers, but Wilfred's video finally gave life to the violent underwater reality of what hunting groupers, Maltese style, entailed. I watched, fascinated, as the divers used their intimate knowledge of the sea to lure these giant groupers out of the caves and then shoot them point-blank, holding on for dear life as the huge fish thrashed and tore against the implanted barbs. "The fish were so plentiful back then," Wilfred explained. "These island boys had been used to fishing with nets from boats, when suddenly they had scuba gear to take them into the groupers' natural environment." Malta's government eventually had to outlaw spearfishing altogether because the groupers became endangered. Wilfred stuck out in a few of the scenes shot by his diver friends, his trademark goatee dark and close-cropped, rather than the bib of gray now framing his chin.

After the video flickered to an end, Wilfred turned off the television and repeated the island's seemingly universal refrain: "You know," he said, "I've lost eight friends in diving accidents over the years." He set the video carefully back in its place and shrugged. "But enough of that," he concluded. "Let me show you some of the treasures I have in my home."

Wilfred's hundred-year-old villa doubled as an archival museum of scuba diving history unlike anything I'd seen in private or public hands. Literally thousands of seaborne artifacts, shells, and bits of diving equipment from his lengthy career sat perched on shelves attached to the patina walls of his home. Among the thousands of samples of undersea flora and fauna I admired were some of the earliest pieces of diving apparatus ever manufactured and used anywhere in the world. I walked past relics of hardhat sponge diving, weathered nautical charts, and bleached shark jaws lined with gleaming teeth. For a moment, I felt as if I'd stepped into a scene from Quint's boathouse in the movie *Jaws*.

When it came to diving, Wilfred had distinguished himself among Malta's diving elite as a brilliant innovator. He showed me, with pride in his eyes, one of the first diving masks ever used in Malta, which he himself created from two strips of an automotive inner tube and a pane of glass. He showed me diving tanks he had fashioned from cylinders scavenged from WWII airplanes and pointed out the first commercially manufactured equipment ever brought to Malta—a 1950s vintage Cousteau Ganon demand valve regulator and Siebe Gorman twin cylinders.

As we continued on, Wilfred disseminated so many facts on such an array of arcane nautical information that my mind could scarcely absorb it. Yet I stopped dead in my tracks when Wilfred offered, almost as an aside, "You know, along with those four anchors you've identified on the Munxar, I've heard of two more taken from shallow waters on the inner reef of the Munxar."

His words struck me like a lightning bolt.

A seemingly innocent remark could well deal a deathblow to a theory I'd spent two years developing. Wilfred seemed surprised when my jaw dropped and I stood staring at the floor. I didn't need to be reminded: The Bible specifically describes *four* anchors being dropped from the stern of Paul's ship. Nowhere does the Bible say "five," or "six," or "three." *Four anchors* were dropped from the stern of Paul's ship off the coast of Malta all those years ago.

More Anchors?

From the first moment, many years ago, when my personal experience taught me that the Bible was a more reliable guide to ancient sites and events than any commentary, atlas, or scholar, God's Word has never let me down. Our research team at the BASE Institute has inevitably found that the best answers to questions of history and archaeology—to say nothing of the issues of life—are found in the pages of Scripture. We have, in fact, been both startled and amazed at how clear, how specific, and how accurate the ancient Hebrew and Greek texts are in describing places, events, and other biblical details that have been inadvertently scrambled by translators and commentators over the years. I knew that, inevitably, the Bible would hold the key to this quandary and that this rumor of two additional anchors would stand or fall with Luke's painstakingly detailed account in Acts 27.

Ray and I discussed the issue at length that night, going over the verses in the Bible, and as I had suspected, the answer lay right in front of our noses all along. Even though the Greek New Testament words for bow and stern are similar, in revisiting the narrative, it became clear that there were certainly more than four anchors aboard Paul's ship.

We had already established that in the teeth of the storm the sailors had dropped four anchors from the stern, or the back of the ship...in *ninety feet* of water. And they dropped them while still some distance from the churning reef that they could hear surging in the darkness, in hopes of keeping the ship from smashing into the rocks.

But then we inspected the following verse, which states that immediately afterward, a small band of sailors, fearing for their lives, pretended to lower "some anchors" from the bow, or the front of the ship. Of course that was it! It hadn't occurred to me before, but there were other anchors onboard the ship in addition to the four they had already let down in the sea.

> *Then fearing lest we should have fallen upon rocks, they cast four anchors out of the stern, and wished for the day. And as the sailors were seeking to escape from the ship, when they had let down the skiff into the sea, under pretense of putting out* anchors *from the prow....*
> (Acts 27:29–30)

There it was again. When the sailors sought to escape from the ship, they did so under the pretense of lowering "anchors from the prow" of the ship, thinking they could get away with lowering the skiff instead. Paul foiled their plan, though, so they remained on the ship and eventually everyone survived.

We went back over the verses to make sure we hadn't misinterpreted the meaning. Since the word *anchors* here is plural (referencing the anchors in the bow), there had to be the prospect of putting out at least *two more* anchors—possibly more—from the bow of the ship. These would be in addition to the four already deployed and holding the ship off the rocks. And, as it turns out, the ancient Roman freighters carried *many* anchors. They were, in fact, the most important gear onboard— and they were invariably stowed in the bow. Given the dire nature of their predicament, if the sailors meant to flee the ship, pretending to drop anchors from the bow would be a logical, albeit deceitful, move. And when their plan didn't work...

> *...the soldiers cut away the ropes of the skiff and let it fall off.* (Acts 27:32)

Now we had to ask ourselves: *Did they manage to drop the anchors into water? Were they in the skiff when it was cut away?* It's impossible to tell, but the word for *pretense* here seems to indicate a totally false motive—the anchors were nothing more than a ruse. The sailors' sole objective was to escape certain death by setting out in the small skiff— not to drop the forward positioned anchors. It's likely that the sailors never even touched the anchors in their escape plot.

This nugget of information had yielded two important new clues: First, the Bible indicates that the four anchors put off the back of the ship were the only four dropped at the fifteen-fathom (or ninety-foot) depth that Luke specified. Second, simple logic dictates that if there had, indeed, been other anchors onboard, they would be found in much shallower water closer to the beach, near where the ship actually struck the reef and went down.

The Munxar Reef trailed out to sea a mile and a half. The four anchors were dropped at the outer tip of the reef and the ship then sailed toward the bay, but they first had to go through the waves crashing over the Munxar. In other words, one could reasonably expect to find *at least* two additional Roman-style anchors (stored in the bow) in much shallower water closer to shore, *between* where the four anchors were deployed and the fatal reef that ultimately shredded and sank the ship.

These two new anchors mentioned by Wilfred should, in fact, have come to rest in a larger debris field, alongside an array of artifacts consistent with a 60 A.D. shipwreck. It all seemed to make sense on paper, but confirming such a scenario would require more time, more investigation, and more interviews. In some ways it felt like starting over.

Little did I know, within two days my answer would mysteriously appear.

Two nights after meeting Wilfred in his home, he called me at my hotel with a curious request. "Bob, I was so captivated by your explanation about why you feel Paul's shipwreck was on the Munxar Reef that I had to call you. I've been diving these waters for over forty years. I know every rock, every current, and every weather pattern. I also know every wreck site, and no one has ever found four anchors dating from the same era at any spot on Malta. Oh, there have been other anchors found, but not at the depths the Bible says and certainly not four together.

"Also, when you read me the verse in the Bible where it says the ship ran aground where two seas meet, it caused me to think and think about what you said. The two seas could only mean the Munxar Reef, because it is there that two currents come together and collide over the reef during a storm."

Wilfred was telling me nothing new. It was a description of the Munxar that had been corroborated in more than twenty interviews. I'd seen it myself: The currents come together over the Munxar. Even though I hadn't seen the waves on the Munxar in a big storm, I'd heard from many of the islanders about the waves on the Munxar creating a surging wall of water extending for more than a mile and a half out to sea. The phenomenon is well-known to divers and fishermen alike. More importantly, their descriptions fit perfectly with Luke's account in Acts 27:41.

Wilfred continued, "I was so intrigued with your theory that I decided to do some snooping around on my own. I talked with several among the small community of old divers on Malta and asked them about the four anchors at your site in the deeper waters of the outer Munxar. They know of the four you speak of, but..." he paused, "as I told you, there's one man who actually found two additional anchors in the shallows on the inner Munxar."

I waited as he cleared his throat and groped for words to explain his phone call.

"I have spoken with this man personally," he continued, "and...he surprised me when he said he wanted to meet with you. These men, these old divers, as you know by now, are a very secretive group. They do not share information easily. But when I told him about your theories, Bob, he said he had a personal reason why he wanted to meet with you."

I listened silently, trying to anticipate where this conversation was headed when Wilfred added, "He does not want to be known. In fact, he wants to meet at an unnamed location. He knows he may go to jail or have a big fine for what he is about to tell you, Bob. He wants to meet tonight, and he wants to tell you of his two anchors he found on the inner Munxar."

Wilfred instructed me to go to the Black Pearl restaurant at 7 P.M. and wait in the parking lot. I agreed and found myself waiting beneath an underhang by the ship docks next to the Black Pearl. The fall evening had turned dark by seven, and the streets were filled with rain from a storm still blowing across the island. I saw Wilfred driving up on a small vintage European scooter. He stopped the scooter in front of me and said, "Get on." I had just left a meeting and was wearing a suit and tie. I must have looked quite a sight, sitting on the back of the scooter, speeding off into the wet night. I had no idea where we were going, and Wilfred seemed cautious, looking behind us on several occasions (I assumed to see if we were being followed).

We pulled up next to a bar that appeared to be closed for the evening. The sign over the door read "The Lucky Bar." Wilfred stopped the motorcycle, and a man wearing a plaid jacket stepped out of the shadows. He approached Wilfred with a swinging limp, and without saying a word, motioned for us to walk across the street to a small coffeehouse.

Once seated in the corner of the coffeehouse, the man quickly lit a cigarette and told me up-front that he didn't want his identity ever made known and demanded assurance that I would never reveal his name. After I agreed, he told the following story:

"Eight years ago I was diving on the Munxar Reef, spearfishing, when a fish darted underneath a rock. I looked under the rock, but I couldn't see the fish. I became frustrated. The fish swam underneath the small outcropping, but I couldn't see it. So I toppled over this rock, wanting only to satisfy my curiosity as to what had happened to the fish."

He talked slowly, seeming to visualize the entire affair in his mind. "I soon forgot about where it had gone, when I saw the straight edge of a large flat form covered in crustaceans. I unsheathed the knife from my leg, scraped the object, and saw the glint of metal. I had heard of other divers finding anchors, about their excitement at that moment, but it was the only anchor I had ever seen in the water. My heart nearly leapt out of my throat when I realized I had actually found a large ancient anchor."

I wanted to know more details—where exactly he had discovered the anchor, how he had brought it to shore—but he stopped me in midsentence.

"I am going to tell you that I found this and another anchor nearby." He paused. "It was also found on the inner Munxar in about ten meters (thirty feet) of water."

I pulled a nautical map from my pocket and asked him to pinpoint the exact location.

"It was eight years ago," he said, "but I know it was definitely in the inner part of the Munxar."

The place he pointed to on the map lay about two hundred or three hundred feet from the spot where I had earlier estimated Paul's ship crashed on the reef. From the site where the four anchors were cut loose on the outer Munxar, it sat a little over three thousand feet in toward the shore in a direct line on the inner reef. Most importantly, he said he found the two anchors at the shallow break in the Munxar Reef, known today as the Munxar Pass. This "pass" would have been the ship's only chance of survival in its desperate attempt to make it to the bay, which was just beyond the inner reef. So it made sense that the sailors would have tried to sail to shore through the small slit in the reef.

His story squared with the rough calculations Ray and I had made two nights earlier. I listened in earnest as the man told me he had heard from Wilfred of my speaking in churches about the Bible; he said he had come offering the information solely to assist in my efforts to tell the whole story.

"When Wilfred told me about all of your research, and how the Munxar lay where the two seas meet," he continued softly, "I couldn't help thinking how all those scholars, all those experts, deciding years ago that the shipwreck occurred in St. Paul's Bay. And they were wrong. I believe you have found the true location of the shipwreck of Paul. I don't know if what I'm telling you will help you or not, but I'm giving you this information, wanting nothing in return." He paused a moment, then added, "I am a religious man, I go to Mass, and I felt I needed to tell you so you could write in your book and speak to many people about the truth of Paul's shipwreck."

"Where are those two anchors today?" I asked, thinking there might be a remote chance of actually seeing the anchors and dating them to the same Roman epoch as the other four.

"I have children," he said, as he bowed his head in a somewhat embarrassed manner. "I sold the anchors for money. I am not proud of this, but this is the way of it. Life is expensive these days, and the fish…a lot of them are gone. It's hard to make a living." The man turned and nodded toward Wilfred, then rose from the table. Our brief meeting was already over. He had told me everything he knew, and it clearly fit the biblical narrative. We shook hands and he left as he had come, walking down the dark street, wet with rain.

Later that evening, as I reflected on our conversation, I replayed in my mind Luke's detailed description of two separate but connected incidents involving the ship's anchors. When the crew had dropped the four anchors from the stern, putting a hard brake on the ship's irresistible crash course toward the reef, another group of frightened sailors had perpetuated their own panicked intrigue. In their failed attempt to flee from the ship, they pretended to lower the forward bow anchors; instead, they ended up casting the lifeboat out to sea.

I found it astonishing that Paul, a prisoner onboard, discerned everything and exposed the crew's plot to the centurion, warning him that, "Unless these men stay in the ship, you cannot be saved." He knew that every sailor would be required to steer that big ship through the treacherous waters where the two seas met if they had any chance of reaching the safety of the bay.

And we all know the rest of story: The ship perished in the violent waves on the reef; the entire crew swam to shore safely; Paul and Luke went on to spread the Good News to a waiting world; and the anchors found their grave in the sand and rocks on the outer waters and the shallows of the inner Munxar Reef, lost to history for more than nineteen centuries.

My purpose here had ended as well. I had followed the trail of the anchors to its outermost reaches; and they, in turn, had spoken to me in soft, whispered secrets from the deep. All that remained was to say thank you to a new family of friends, bid farewell to exquisite Malta, and return home. ⚓

Chapter Eighteen

THE ANCHOR
OF OUR HOPE

*O*n my final day in Malta, I walked out to the edge of the sheer cliffs above the Munxar Reef. Standing there, I stared at the foaming waves breaking upon the rocks below. The storm during the past week had stirred the sea into mounting swells that were now merging together over the reef. The waves were fairly modest, nothing like you would see in a northeaster, where huge waves crash together sending plumes of spray forty or more feet into the air. The currents that carried these swells on their long journey to the southeast shore of Malta arrived from different directions, peeling upon themselves, offering a perfect portrait of what the Bible describes as "a place where two seas meet."

As I watched the waves swell and melt away, I reflected on my long journey's end. I thought of strong, big-hearted Tony diving down on this reef, to his "Bank," where the big groupers lay. My thoughts traveled to the unique fraternity of divers I met on my several trips to Malta and their colorful stories recalling the thrilling moment when the anchors pulled free from the grip of the seafloor and rose to the surface in a swirl of sand and excitement. I also thought of the apostle Paul and his exhausted fellow shipmates, clawing their way to the sandy shore below me. Sitting there, I wondered... *What* other *clues might still be hidden in the shroud of sand below the churning currents at the place where "two seas meet?"*

When I started the Malta project, I thought it would be a simple process: Go to the place Luke describes in the Bible, hire a boat, dive down, find the anchors, and then bring them up. I would follow an old storm that spoke a lost message written on the waves of time and the ancient pages of the Bible. I hoped that the Mediterranean had kept these anchors hidden for almost two thousand years under a protective canopy of sea. Ninety feet below, they would quietly wait for me to come along and wake them from their long slumber.

But, more than three decades before I started my search, several young Maltese spear fishermen got there first. With rubber and glass masks on their faces and metal cylinders of compressed air lashed to their backs, they dove down into the clear blue sea, discovering an archaeo-logical find that I believe is of monumental importance. There, stuck in the sand, in front of St. Thomas Bay out on the Munxar reef, lay a cluster of huge lead Roman anchor stocks in a tangle of swaying seaweed.

These divers, however, didn't even consider that those artifacts could have been from the lost ship of Paul. The legend of Paul ship-wrecking in St. Paul's Bay had existed for so long that it was indelibly etched in the Maltese culture, and consequently, anchors produced from any other bay could not be seen as being from Paul's ship. According to the long-standing tradition, Paul's ship went down in St.

Paul's Bay, and no other bay was even considered by those that discovered these ancient lead treasures.

By the time I arrived in Malta, the anchors were gone, removed from their sandy graves by young men who didn't even know the significance of what they had found. I consider it a blessing, however, that I wasn't the one to dive down and discover those anchors lying on the seafloor. Circumstances shielded me from the temptation of saying "I discovered." I did not pull anything from the sea and now can only point to the incredible accuracy of Luke's narrative and say, "These are the facts and they all line up."

For me, that is the greatest discovery I could ever hope to make.

Standing alone on the cliffs overlooking St. Thomas Bay, I wondered, *Why did Paul and the rest of those men on that Alexandrian grain freighter have to endure such incredible hardship? Didn't Jesus Himself tell Paul in a vision just prior to the voyage, "You must go to Rome"?* Certainly God, who controls all things, could have prevented that storm and calmed the seas; He could have made sweet, warm winds that would nudge the ship to Rome.

What was the meaning of that storm, of that frightful shipwreck?

Suddenly it occurred to me—the prisoners who survived that shipwreck, and who drew strength from Paul's heroic words, would go on to tell this miraculous story to other prisoners they encountered. The ship's owner, witness to the miracle of his own salvation at sea, would relate the tale to the aristocracy of Rome. The sailors would travel on to distant lands, everywhere speaking of their deliverance and of the Jewish slave who spoke to angels and served this man called Jesus. The soldiers no doubt carried the Good News of Christ down the long dusty roads leading to military campaigns in far-off frontiers. Through a terrible storm, from the ruins of a shipwreck, Paul's story would be carried on the lips of seafaring travelers the world over.

We have often thought of Paul as a solitary messenger chosen by the Lord to battle against all odds and fulfill the task of spreading the Gospel. But in the vast, unknowable economy of God, it had been ordained that *many* would carry the message of hope abroad. Through this humble story, I pray that the message about our one true Anchor—the Person of our eternal hope—will resonate once again across the globe, from a certain island called Malta. ⚓

AFTERWORD

*T*he anchor stocks described in this book are prized by the families who inherited them from the sea. These lead artifacts are also recognized by all involved as belonging to the historical heritage of the country of Malta.

As of the printing of this book, the fate of the surviving anchors are as follows:

Two of the anchors have been turned over to officials at the Malta Museum, generous gifts given in memory of Tony by his wife Margaret and his friend Charles Grech.

The family of "Mario the diver" is involved in meaningful dialogue to determine an appropriate disposition of that ancient treasure.

And the weathered dive weight that had been melted down from the torn-in-half anchor found by Tony and Ray sits in front of me as I type these final words—the chiseled "MT" indelibly etched on its dull gray surface.

A presidential pardon has been signed by the President and Prime Minister of Malta, giving amnesty to those persons who possessed the anchor stocks found on the seabed in St. Thomas Bay. The order from the President is as follows:

ORDNI

MILL-PRESIDENT TA' MALTA

LIL KULL MIN HUWA KONĊERNAT

BILLI ġie rakkomandat lili mill-Ministru responsabbli għall-Kultura illi tingħata maħfra lill-persuni illi għandhom fill-pussess tagħhom oġġetti ta' antikità li għandhom importanza ġeoloġika, paleontoliġika, arkeoloġika, ta' qdumija jew artistika misjuba f'kull żmien f'qiegħ il-baħar fl-ibħra territorjali Maltin inkluż is-sikka tal-Munxar fil-Bajja ta' San Tumas limiti ta' Marsaskala Malta, u li qegħdin iżommu l-istess oġġetti bi ksur ta' l-Att dwar il-Protezzjoni tal-Antikitajiet (Kap 54) jew ta' l-Att Dwar il-Patrimonju Kulturali (Kap 445) jew ta' xi liġi oħra u illi din il-maħfra tingħata taħt il-kondizzjoni illi l-oġġetti imsemmija jiġu ritornati, konsenjati u permanentement ċeduti bla ħlas lill-Gvern, jew direttament mill-persuni illi għandhom dawk l-oġġetti jew permezz ta' xi intermedjarju, sa mhux aktar tard minn sittin (60) jum mid-data ta' din il-maħfra, u dan sabiex tingħata l-opportunità illi l-istess oġġetti jidħlu fil-pussess ta' l-awtoritajiet inkarigati illi jieħdu ħsieb il-wirt storiku u antikwarju Malti u dawn il-każijiet jiġu riżolti.

U BILLI jiena naqbel ma' din ir-rakkomandazzjoni.

JIENA ISSA GĦALHEKK, Guido de Marco, President ta' Malta, bis-saħħa tas-setgħat mogħtija lili bl-Artikolu 93 tal-Kostituzzjoni,
B'DAN NORDNA li tingħata maħfra lill-persuni li fi żmien sittin (60) jum mid-data ta' din il-maħfra jirritornaw, jikkonsenjaw u permanentement iċedu bla ħlas lill-Ministru responsabbli għall-Kultura, direttament jew permezz ta' intermedjarju, oġġetti ta' antikità li għandhom importanza ġeoloġika, paleontoloġika, arkeoloġika, ta' qdumija jew artistika misjuba f'kull żmien f'qiegħ il-baħar fl-ibħra territorjali Maltin inkluż is-sikka tal-Munxar fil-Bajja ta' San Tumas limiti ta' Marsaskala, Malta illi huma jkunu iddetjenew bi ksur ta' l-Att dwar il-Protezzjoni tal-Antikitajiet (Kap 54) jew ta' l-Att dwar il-Patrimonju Kulturali (Kap 445) jew ta' xi liġi oħra u dan rigward kull reat u/jew kull responsabilità kriminali riżultanti mill-istess detenzjoni, sejbien jew tfittxija ta' l-oġġetti in kwistjoni.

Din l-ordni tibda sseħħ fil- **23** ta' Settembru 2002.

U għal dan il-għan din hija awtorità biżżejjed

Magħmul il-Palazz, Valletta
Illum **23** ta' Settembru tas-sena
Elfejn u tnejn

PRESIDENT TA' MALTA

B'AWTORITÀ

PRIM MINISTRU

To whom it may concern:

Since it has been recommended by the Minister responsible for Culture, that a presidential pardon be granted to those persons who have in their possession antique objects having a geological, palaeontological, archaeological, antiquarian or artistic importance, found during any time in the seabed in St. Thomas Bay limits of Marsascala, Malta and who are detaining, maintaining the said objects in breach of the Antiquities (Protection) Act (Chapter 54) or the Cultural Heritage Act (Chapter 445) or of any other law and that the said presidential pardon be granted under the condition that the items mentioned be returned, consigned and permanently handed over to the Minister responsible for culture, whether directly by the persons who are in possession of the said objects or through intermediaries, 60 days from the date of this pardon, and this so as to give the opportunity for the competent authorities be given possession of the said objects, which authorities are responsible for Maltese Cultural Heritage and antiquarian, and this in order to resolve these cases.

And since I agree with the above recommendation.

I, Gwido De Marco, President of Malta, therefore, in virtue of the powers given to me by Section 93 of the Maltese Constitution, hereby order that a pardon is granted to those persons who, within 60 days from the date of this presidential pardon, return, consign and permanently hand over to the Minister responsible for Culture, directly or through intermediaries, objects having a geological, palaeontological, archaeological, antiquarian or artistic importance, found during any time in the seabed in St. Thomas Bay limits of Marsascala, Malta and who are detaining, maintaining the said objects in breach of the Antiquities (Protection) Act (Chapter 54) or the Cultural Heritage Act (Chapter 445) or of any other law in relation to any offence resulting from the said detention, discovery or research for the said objects.

This order shall be valid as from the 23rd September 2002.
Signed on the 23rd September 2002 by the Prime Minister and the President of Malta.

ACKNOWLEDGMENTS

*W*hat started out as a simple project transformed into several years of an intense commitment of time, effort, and money. It became a labor of love. Any successes resulting from my efforts can only be attributed to those who assisted, guided, and encouraged me along the way. Words could never express the deep appreciation I have for the those kind and generous individuals who made this story possible.

TERRY CORNUKE, EDGAR & YVONNE MILES,

JERRY AND GAIL NORDSKOG, BOB YERKES,

DAVID & PENNY BERGLUND, JIM & ROBIN DaPRA,

JIM AND LAURRA FITZGERALD, KATHY PROFFITT,

JASON MILLIKEN, DAVID HALBROOK, KATHERINE LLOYD,

JENNIFER GOTT, PAM LONGO, BARBARA HONTS,

RAY & CAROLE ARDIZZONE, PETE & BARBARA LEININGER,

MIKE & SUSAN BARNES, RON & DEBY ACTON,

KEN DURHAM, J. O. STEWART, DARRELL & SANDY SCOTT,

RON & TISHA HICKS, DOUG SCHERLING,

CHUCK & NANCY MISSLER, PAUL & NANCY CORNUKE,

JERRY ROSE, MARK & ANGELA PHILLIPS,

MITCH YELLEN, DAVE LADELL, GARY SMELTZER,

JEAN FRANCOIS LAARCHEVEC, GEORGE KRALIK,

BRYAN BOORUJY, DAVID STOTTS, JOHN DOUGLAS,

TOM & KIM BENGARD, GARY & LISA BACKSTROM,

LIONEL CASSON, JIM & PENNY CALDWELL,

JOHN & REGINA CORNUKE, JOEL FREEMAN,

ROY KNUTESON, NORM & CAROLE SONJU,

STEVE MEYER, JOSH MCDOWELL, GENE HANSON,

BRUCE HENDERSON, BILL & SUSAN HENRY,

LEN SALVIG, JACOB CAROTTA, JOYCE WILKINS,

HIS EXCELLENCY PROFESSOR GUIDO DE MARCO,

PRIME MINISTER EDDIE FENECH ADAMI, RAY CIANCIO,

JO PALMER, LOUIS GALEA, MICHAEL RAFELO,

MARGARET MICALLEF-BORG, PAUL GUILLAUMIER,

JOANNE MICALLEF, JOE MICALLEF, CHARLIE VELLA,

JOE NAVARRO, OLIVER NAVARRO, CHARLES GRECH,

WILFRED PIRROTTA, GENERAL RUPERT MONTANARO,

MAJOR MANUEL MALLIA, JAMES MULHOLLAND,

JETHRO MULHOLLAND, MRS. "MARIO",

PROFESSOR ANTHONY BONANNO, PAUL PRECA TRAPANI,

JOHN PRECA TRAPANI, ROGER MAGRO, LE LI, SUE,

MICHAEL & EMMA, MARK MICELI FARRUGIA,

MEDITERRANEAN FILM STUDIOS,

HUGH PERALTA, NOELLA GRIMA,

AQUA BUBBLES DIVING SCHOOL,

JAMES REID, KEVIN BRYAN, JOE & NOAH RITCHIE,

HEATHER MERCER, DAYNA CURRY,

LINDY BOOK, MARY IRWIN VICKERS,

JOHN & REBECCA JACKSON, MISGANNA,

JOHN MCGEE, RON & ANN NEILSON, MARK BRIGHT,

BRETT & JAMIE RUDOLPH, ELIZABETH RIDENOUR,

DIANA SCHNIEDER, LARRY WILLIAMS,

BOB & CAROL WALLACE, BILL & NANCY ZARELLA,

AL & RONNIE FUSTER, PAUL FEINBERG

NOTES

1. Comm. Salvino Athony Scicluna. K. M., *Shipwreck of St. Paul: Conclusions of Underwater Researches by the Malta Underwater Archaeological Branch of the International Institute of Mediterranean Underwater Archaeology, Teams from the Royal Navy, the Royal Air Force, and the Army. 1961-85* (Malta, 1985), 18.

2. Giueseppe Castelli and Charles Cini, *Malta Romana Il Patrimonio Archeologico Delle Isole Maltesi* (1992), 25. "Salina Bay too must have served as a small harbour since it appears to have hosted some harbour activity in antiquity judging from a number of lead anchors in or just outside it."

3. Ibid., 26–8.

4. The explorations focused on two prime areas of St. Paul's Bay: Mistra Bay and Tal Azzenin. The findings, summarized in the published report titled *In Search of St. Paul* by Specialists Archaeological Systems, Malta, revealed nothing relating to first-century shipping or shipwrecks in Mistra Bay. Concerning Tal Azzenin, the report concluded that "…the conditions necessary for a wrecking to occur on Tal Azzenin combined with the type of storm necessary to take ships on the reef would be rarer than immediately expected. Any ship would have already had to negotiate either a passage around St. Paul's Islands or around Qawra Point, and the nonce in the relative security of the bay be brought on to the reef." There have also been theories about Qawra Point— also situated along the same familiar coastline—but numerous problems eliminate its consideration. Not only would the coastline features have been easily recognized by sailors accustomed to navigating by visual reckoning rather than maps; its seafloor contours do not match the depth soundings recorded by Luke as the ship approached the island. As recorded in the Specialists Archaeological Systems report, "The situation of the topography

of the area, combined with the shallow depth of less than five metres for at least one hundred metres around much of the promontory, suggest that this would have seen the foundering of many ships.... The nature of the seabed and the scatter of durable artifacts over a wide area suggest that many ships [and anchors] have been lost [here] in the past." The anchors that have been located in this area are of varying sizes, varying dates, and from depths inconsistent with Luke's record. The evidence is more consistent with a well-visited port outside of which numerous ships throughout the centuries ran aground and sank. A search of nearby Mellieha Bay also produced nothing of significance.

5. Readers Digest, *Strange Stories Amazing Facts* (Readers Digest Association Inc., 1976), 330.

6. See http://members.tripod.com/~S_van_Dorst/legio.html#officers.

7. F. F. Bruce, *Paul: Apostle of the Heart Set Free* (Grand Rapids, Mich.: Wm B. Eerdmans, 1977), 369.

8. Ibid., 368.

9. Lionel Casson, *Ships and Seafaring in Ancient Times* (Austin, Tex.: University of Texas Press, 1994), 124.

10. Ibid., 123.

11. Jefferson White, *Evidence and Paul's Journeys: An Historical Investigation into the Travels of the Apostle Paul* (Hilliard, Ohio: Parsagard Press, 2001), 71.

12. "The Saga of the Lady Be Good" at http://bbs.macmad.org/~jamiecox/ladybegood/ ladybegood.html.

13. *The Great Siege: Passport's Illustrated Guide to Malta and Gozo* (Passports Books, 2000), 90.

14. A. T. Robertson, *A Grammar of the Greek New Testament in the Light of Historical Research* (Nashville, Tenn.: Broadman Press, 1934), 1020–1. This type of construction occurs only eleven times in the New Testament. The

phrase eiv du,nainto appears in Acts 27:39 alone and incorporates the use of ei; plus the optative mood in the protasis, meeting the requirements for a fourth class conditional clause. Earlier in Acts, Luke uses the phrase ei; pwj du,nainto in 27:12, but adds the particle pwj meaning "somehow," indicating that though reaching Phoenix was a "future least probable" long shot, it could still be "somehow" or "in some way" possible. As it turned out, it was not possible.

15. H. G. Liddell and R. Scott, *Greek-English Lexicon* (Oxford, England: Clarendon Press, 1996).

16. Thayer's Lexicon as derived from Grimms Lexicon of 1889.

17. According to *Sport Diving: The British Sub-Aqua Club Diving Manual* (London: Ebury Press, 1993), 146, "The use of compressed air for lifting heavy objects was pioneered by Cox and Danks in Scapa Flow during the 1920s. Vessels as large as 26,000-ton battleships were raised using the natural buoyancy of the upturned ships after the holes had been plugged and they had been filled with air."

18. Another witness to other witnesses described the anchor as literally being cut in two, as if the anchor had been cut by a hacksaw.

19. *Archaeology and Fertility Cult in the Ancient Mediterranean,* and *Religion and Society in the Prehistoric Mediterranean.* Professor Bonanno has also authored various publications on Roman Art and Maltese Archaeology. Among some of the more important are *Malta: An Archaeological Paradise* (Malta, 1987); *Excavations at Hal Millieri, Malta,* a report on the excavation campaign conducted on behalf of the National Museum of Malta (coauthor and coeditor with T. F. C. Blagg and A. T. Luttrell, University of Malta Press, 1990); *Roman Malta: The Archaeological Heritage of the Maltese Islands* (Rome, 1992).

20. *The Harper Collins Atlas of the Bible* (London: Times Books Limited, 1998), 173.

21. Lloyd J. Ogilvie, *The Communicator's Commentary: Acts* (Waco, Tex.: Word Books, 1983), 335.

22. Casson, *Ships and Seafaring in Ancient Times,* 103–4.

23. Synesius, *Epistolae,* 4.160a, as cited in Casson, *Ships and Seafaring in Ancient Times,* 129.

24. Josephus, *The Life of Flavius Josephus,* 3.15, as published in *The New Complete Works of Josephus* (Grand Rapids, Mich.: Kregel Publications, 1999), 18.

25. Alan Millard, *Illustrated Wonders and Discoveries of the Bible* (Nashville, Tenn.: Thomas Nelson), 211.

26. J. D. Douglas, organizing ed., *The New Bible Dictionary* (Grand Rapids, Mich.: Wm B. Eerdmans, 1974), 945.